The Mean in Budgeting

Yannan Gou

The Mean in Budgeting

Insights from Chinese Confucian Principles

中国财经出版传媒集团
中国财政经济出版社

Springer

Yannan Gou
Shanghai University
Shanghai, China

Translated by
Qiaolian Zhu
Shanghai University
Shanghai, China

ISBN 978-981-96-9591-1 ISBN 978-981-96-9592-8 (eBook)
https://doi.org/10.1007/978-981-96-9592-8

Jointly published with China Financial & Economic Publishing House
The print edition is not for sale in The Mainland of China. Customers from The Mainland of China please order the print book from: China Financial & Economic Publishing House
ISBN of the Co-Publisher's edition: 978-7-5223-0966-8

This Springer imprint is published by the registered company Springer Nature Singapore Pte Ltd.
The registered company address is: 152 Beach Road, #21-01/04 Gateway East, Singapore 189721, Singapore

Budgetary Insights from Zhu Xi's Preface to *Zhongyong Zhangju*

[Zhu Xi] Why was the *Zhongyong* (The Doctrine of the Mean) written? It was composed by Zisi (circa 481–402 BCE), the esteemed grandson of Confucius (circa 551–479 BCE), out of concern that the teachings of the Dao (Way) might lose their transmission. Since the ancient sage-kings inherited the Mandate of Heaven and established the highest standards, the transmission of the Way has had its origins. Within the Confucian canon, the concept of "adhering to the mean" was articulated by the sage-king Yao when he abdicated the throne in favor of Shun (Yao and Shun are revered as two of the legendary Five Emperors of antiquity). Another profound statement, "The mind of man is precarious; the mind aligned with the Way is subtle. Only with precision and focus can one adhere to the mean." was pronounced when Shun transferred power to Yu the Great (the founder of the Xia Dynasty, circa 2070-1600 BCE). Yao's singular declaration encapsulates the principles in their entirety. Shun's subsequent elucidations further expound upon Yao's wisdom, asserting that true comprehension of the doctrine is attainable only through grasping these intricate connections.*

[Zhu Xi] I have previously expounded upon this: the ethereal and perceptive nature of the mind is a singular, inherent quality. The distinction between the human mind and the mind aligned with the Way arises from their origins—either from the individual's physical form and temperament or from the pure nature of the heavenly mandate. Thus, the governing principles of perception differ: they may be dangerous and restless, or subtle and difficult to manifest. However, no one can exist without this physical form, so even the wisest cannot be without the human mind; and everyone possesses this nature, so even the most foolish cannot be without the mind aligned with the Way. These two are intermingled, and without proper regulation, the dangerous will become more perilous, and the subtle will become increasingly elusive. The great and selfless heavenly principle will never be able to overcome selfish human desires. By being precise, one can distinguish between the two without conflating them; by being focused, one can maintain the purity of one's original mind without deviation. Through continuous practice, the mind aligned with the Way will always govern the body, and the human mind will comply in all matters. Thus, the dangerous will become tranquil, the subtle will become manifest, and actions and speech will naturally be without excess or deficiency.*

The Way of budgeting is encapsulated in the concept "adhering to the mean", signifying the importance of maintaining balance in response to varying historical contexts. Adhering to the mean, the bedrock of budgeting, ensures long-term stability and transcends specific time periods or events.

The neglect of the Way can lead to potential risks, while its adherence promotes stability and security. Budgeting is influenced by a multitude of factors, including political, economic, cultural, traditional, and environmental elements. Participants in the budgeting process may exhibit varying degrees of objectivity and bias. Micro-level correctness may lead to macro-level fallacies, and vice versa. Therefore, the budgeting process necessitates a return to correct principles, procedures, and operations to fulfill its intended role.

[Zhu Xi] Yao, Shun, and Yu were illustrious sages who ascended to the throne. The transfer of the mandate to rule the world is a matter of profound significance. As sages who became emperors, they performed great deeds for the benefit of all under heaven, and at the moment of their transition, their admonitions were of the utmost gravity. Is there any principle in the world more exalted than this? From that time onward, the transmission of the Way continued from sage to sage. Kings such as Cheng Tang of the Shang Dynasty (circa 1600-1046 BCE), King Wen of the late Shang, and King Wu of the Zhou Dynasty (circa 1046-256 BCE), along with ministers like Gao Yao, Yi Yin of the Shang, Fu Yue of the Shang, the Duke of Zhou, and the Duke of Shao of the Zhou, all upheld these few words to perpetuate the Way. As for our Master, Confucius, though he did not attain the position of emperor, he inherited the teachings of the ancient sages, pioneered new paths, and instructed later scholars. His achievements even surpassed those of Yao and Yu. During his time, the true essence of the teachings was comprehended and transmitted only by his disciples Yan Hui and Zeng Shen. When Zeng's teachings were passed down to Confucius' grandson, Zisi, deviations from the original teachings began to emerge. Zisi, fearing that the true essence would be lost over time, traced back the intentions handed down from Yao and Shun, verified them with the teachings he had received from his father and teachers, and elaborated on them to create this book for future scholars. His deep concern led to earnest words; his far-reaching considerations resulted in detailed explanations.*

Budgeting, shaped by both mindset and circumstance, is not a one-time solution due to the dynamic nature of both elements. It faces ongoing challenges and contradictions. Stability in budgeting can only be achieved through risk awareness, comprehensive consideration, and optimization of institutional development, organizational structure, and procedural arrangements. Effectiveness in budgeting requires exploration of deep-seated principles, steadfastness in strategic planning, project selection, and standard formulation, and consideration of long-term and systemic factors.

[Zhu Xi] "Conforming to the innate nature bestowed by Heaven" pertains to the mind aligned with the Way. "Choosing the good and steadfastly adhering to it" signifies preciseness and focus. "The Noble Man adheres to it" denotes adherence to the mean.*

Effective governance is a prerequisite for successful budgeting, and conversely, ineffective budgeting can impede governance. The Way of budgeting necessitates comprehension, decision-making, persistence, and discernment of the essence amidst change. It demands continual reassessment, reselection, and long-term steadfastness.

[Zhu Xi] *Zhongyong*, enduring for over a millennium, retains its precision and truth. No other sage texts offer such clarity and comprehensiveness in logical organization and profound truth revelation. Zisi transmitted this work to Mencius (circa 371–289 BCE), who further understood and elaborated this work, inheriting the ancient sages' legacy. However, in post-Mencius era, the teachings' prominence waned. The doctrine's essence was metaphorically embedded in texts, while heretical views evolved, being misleading and deviating from the true Confucian way, as seen in Daoist and Buddhist teachings. Fortunately, *Zhongyong* survived, enabling the Cheng brothers (Masters Cheng Hao and Cheng Yi, influential Neo-Confucian philosophers of the Song Dynasty in China) to continue Confucius' teachings and refute the seemingly persuasive arguments of Daoism and Buddhism. Zisi's contributions were significant, but without the Cheng brothers, his thoughts would not have transformed into profound insights. Regrettably, the Cheng brothers' teachings were not widely disseminated, and the records compiled by Shi Jie (1034–1105, a disciple and friend of the Cheng brothers) were limited to the Cheng school disciples. While the Cheng brothers' basic concepts are clear, in-depth analysis is lacking.*

The history of budgeting is marked by the evolution of budgetary concepts and practices, and the conflict of budgetary ideologies and measures. Political aspirations and economic pressures often dictate the trajectory of budgeting, with political ideals supplanting careful consideration, and expedient actions masquerading as transformative innovations. Some rigidly adhere to established norms, while others go with prevailing trends.

Various budgetary ideologies cyclically gain prominence, each purporting to be the truth, but often abruptly ending. As circumstances evolve, so must guiding principles and ideologies, with the Way of budgeting being the pivotal factor shaping these changes.

[Zhu Xi] The Cheng school had diverse and dynamic interpretations. Many of them were based on personal insights and experiences, and some even departed from the original teachings and incorporated elements from Daoism and Buddhism.*

[Zhu Xi] During my early years, I diligently studied *Zhongyong* and encountered many questions. I contemplated them incessantly for several years. After a sudden realization, I seemed to grasp the essence of the book and wrote the *Zhongyong Zhangju* (Commentaries on the Doctrine of the Mean), drawing on the strengths of various schools of thought and hoping for future corrections. Together with a few of my students, we re-examined the book of Shi Jie, removing its complexities and confusions, and named it "Abridged Edition". In the appendix to the *Zhongyong Zhangju*, I included my answers and clarifications on various questions raised regarding *Zhongyong*. Consequently, the purpose, structure, coherence, and analysis of *Zhongyong* are all elaborately presented. The similarities and differences among various schools of thought, as well as their merits and shortcomings, are also expressed tactfully, facilitating comparison and appreciation. Although I dare not claim this pertains to the transmission of the Way, it might be useful for those who are new to studying *Zhongyong*, and perhaps offer some help to those who wish to continue advancing.*

[Zhu Xi] This preface was composed by Zhu Xi in Xin'an (Anhui Province) in the spring of the year 1189 under Emperor Chunxi of the Southern Song Dynasty (1127–1279).*

Budgeting is a complex process that requires testing by practice. Short-term benefits are not sufficient for long-term success, and long-term objectives demand current actions. What factors enable budgetary measures that are feasible, sustainable, acceptable, and rational in the short and long run? The answer to this question will reveal the Way that informs the decision-making process in budgeting.

Note: The paragraphs marked with an asterisk (*) are sourced from Zhu Xi's *Sishu Zhangju Jizhu* (Collected Commentaries on the Four Books), specifically *Zhongyong Zhangju* (Commentaries on the Zhongyong), Preface, pages 14–16.

Shanghai, China
August 2021

Yannan Gou

Preface

Throughout the history of contemporary fiscal planning, a myriad of budgetary paradigms has been introduced, most of which originated from the west. However, the effectiveness of these budgetary models is often time-bound, tailored to work best within certain contexts.

To truly grasp the Way of budgeting is to identify an enduring framework for the application of budgetary concepts and principles. The adage "One cannot make bricks without straw" holds particularly true in an era of tight budgets, when the need to delve into reasoning and take timely action is crucial.

In the search for the answer, I have tried to seek enlightenment in Chinese classics, dedicating two decades to the study of the *Zhongyong* (The Doctrine of the Mean). The depth of its wisdom is boundless. In my twenty-year budgetary work, I have engaged in introspection and practical application of its profound teachings, which continues to yield fresh insights daily, instilling in me a perpetual sense of caution and prudence.

In 1998, my professional journey commenced in the budget office, where budgeting became my primary focus. Each numerical figure and each budgetary item were meticulously scrutinized. Each statement and each report were subjected to rigorous contemplation. Those acquainted with my passion would greet this revelation with a knowing smile, while others may remain oblivious to the depth of my pursuit.

In 2004, at the China Executive Leadership Academy in Pudong, I discovered the multifaceted nature of budgeting. To executives, it was a catalyst for noble causes, a motivator through strategic fund allocation, and a tool for fair benefit distribution. Budgeting was recognized as a political instrument, needing political context for accuracy, and a technological process, requiring robust tech support for reliability.

Starting 2014, as a university budget officer, I began to immerse myself in the annual cycle of budgeting, implementation and improvement. This involved analyzing income (current, potential, and additional sources), expenditures (permissible and non-permissible), and the implications of no expenses.

I tackled budgetary responsibility, accountability, and the nature of this accountability. I navigated the budgetary preparation, decision-making, implementation, auditing, evaluation, and improvement strategies. Despite changes in budget planners, the essence of budgetary work remained constant.

As we transition into a new era, the scope of budgeting extends beyond its traditional confines. The outbreak of the COVID-19 pandemic, shifts in the international landscape, and adjustments in national strategies have precipitated transformations in budgetary practices.

In the face of escalating uncertainty, there is an imperative for budgets to be more flexible and proactive. However, the dichotomy between income and expenditure is intensifying, constricting the budgetary space. The expenditure security comes at the cost of budgetary risks.

Contemporary budgeting can be likened to a shackled elephant attempting to dance—perpetually bracing for potential impacts from various quarters, shouldering the burden of addressing significant issues, laboriously maintaining equilibrium, and advancing with considerable difficulty.

The inquiry into the Way of budgeting was born out of an in-depth study of the *Zhongyong* with esteemed colleagues Xiangchen, Lin Hui, Junfeng, Zhifeng, Xuyuan, and Liuxun. The joy derived from intellectual discourse with like-minded individuals is indeed delightful. Despite previous readings of this book, the profundity and enjoyment experienced during this collaborative dissection of the text was unparalleled, leading to the idea of utilizing classical works to substantiate personal viewpoints.

Specifically, I endeavored to scrutinize budgeting through the lens provided by the *Zhongyong*. Initially, the working title of the book was "Interpreting Budgeting through the Lens of Zhongyong". Drawing from the *Sishu Zhangju Jizhu* 四书章句集注 (Collected Commentaries on the Four Books), specifically *Zhongyong Zhangju* (Commentaries on the Doctrine of the Mean) by the Chinese philosopher Zhu Xi (1130–1200), I composed a budgetary analysis for each of the thirty-three chapters, articulating my thoughts candidly, with the aim of encapsulating my decades of experience.

Upon completion of the initial draft, I sought the counsel of my friend Zhifeng, who advocated meticulous analysis of each sentence and the inner logic of the classic. Consequently, I embarked on a fresh endeavor, parsing each sentence and penning my understanding in the context of budgeting.

The current title of the book, "The Mean in Budgeting: Insights from Chinese Confucian Principles", signifies that budgeting should adhere to principle of the mean, uphold justice, prioritize the well-being of people, promote high-quality development, and prevent systemic risks. Budgeting should also strike a balance between control and performance, adhere to virtuous principles, engage in regular introspection, and strive for a state of equilibrium and harmony.

A formidable journey can be accomplished through incremental progress. After two years of intermittent composition, the manuscript has finally reached fruition. In reflecting upon this odyssey, I find a resonant echo in the closing verses of 'Faust'.

All earth comprises
Is symbol alone;
What there ne'er suffices
As fact here is known;
All past the humanly
Wrought here in love;
The Eternal-Womanly
Draws us above.

Shanghai, China
August 2021

Yannan Gou

The Doctrine of the Mean in Budgeting

[Zhu Xi] The term *zhong* (中) signifies following the mean or the middle course, leaning neither to one side nor the other, neither excessive nor deficient. The term *yong* (庸) means maintaining the normal or constant.*

[Zhu Xi] The Masters Cheng said "Following the mean is the essence of *zhong*, while being unchanging is the essence of *yong*. *Zhong* constitutes the right way to follow for all under heaven; *Yong* constitutes the universal principle regulating all under heaven." This text embodies the Confucian teachings of the mind, transmitted from one generation to another within the Confucian school. Fearing errors should arise over time, Zisi compiled these teachings into a book, known as *Zhongyong*, and entrusted it to his disciple Mencius. The book begins with a single principle, then expands to encompass all things, and finally returns to unify them under that one principle. When unrolled, it fills the universe; when rolled up, it retreats into mystery. Its essence is inexhaustible. The entire work is a treasure trove of profound knowledge. A skillful reader, upon thoroughly exploring and understanding it, can apply its teachings throughout their life, finding its wisdom endless.*

The budget reflects the execution of political choices, the equilibrium between income and expenditure, and the allocation of benefits. Politics has a vital role in shaping the budget, and political legitimacy is a necessary condition for a sound budget. The budget supports the operation of politics, and a prudent and rational budget constitutes the basis of good governance.

Excessive tax that burdens the people is untenable, while inadequate revenue hampers the government's ability to deliver basic public services and address major practical demands and the people's voice. Only by adhering to the mean and avoiding excesses can resources be efficiently distributed, meeting the needs of both the government and the market, and securing a stable and sustainable budget.

Note: The paragraphs marked with an asterisk (*) are sourced from Zhu Xi's *Sishu Zhangju Jizhu* (Collected Commentaries on the Four Books), specifically *Zhongyong Zhangju* (Commentaries on the Zhongyong), pre-Chap. 1, page 17.

Contents

1 **The Way of Budgeting** 1
2 **The Changes in Budgeting** 7
3 **The Challenges of Budgeting** 11
4 **The Reality of Budgeting** 15
5 **The Ideals of Budgeting** 19
6 **The Balance in Budgeting** 21
7 **The Consistency in Budgeting** 23
8 **The Principles of Budgeting** 27
9 **The Justice in Budgeting** 29
10 **The Strength of Budgeting** 31
11 **The Common Sense of Budgeting** 35
12 **The Rationality in Budgeting** 39
13 **Budgeting with People in Mind** 43
14 **Within Budget** 47
15 **Collaboration in Budgeting** 51
16 **Beyond Budgeting** 55
17 **The Essence of Budgeting** 59
18 **The Budget Cycle** 63
19 **The Traditions of Budgeting** 67
20 **The Budget System** 73
21 **The Return to Budgeting** 87

22 The Logic of Budgeting ... 91

23 The Improvement of Budgeting ... 93

24 The Practice of Budgeting ... 95

25 Budget Performance ... 97

26 Budget Governance ... 101

27 Budget Strategies ... 107

28 The Era of Budgeting ... 111

29 The Gains and Losses of Budgeting ... 115

30 The Politics of Budgeting ... 121

31 The Framework of Budgeting ... 125

32 The Government in Budgeting ... 129

33 The Vision of Budgeting ... 133

Bibliography ... 141

Chapter 1
The Way of Budgeting

[Zhongyong] What Heaven mandates is termed "nature". Conforming to this nature is termed "the Way". Cultivating the Way is termed "education".

[Commentary] "Mandate" is similar to "order", while "nature" is akin to "principle". Heaven employs the interaction of the *yin* and *yang* and the Five Elements to engender all things, bestowing upon them forms through the aid of *qi* (vital energy) and assigning them principle, similar to an order. Thus, human beings are born, each with their assigned principle, with the goal of promoting Five Virtues (i.e., benevolence, righteousness, propriety, wisdom, and trustworthiness). This is what we term "nature". "The Way" resembles a path or road. If each individual adheres to their innate nature, they will always take the proper path in their day-to-day activities. This is what we call "the Way". "To cultivate" means to regulate. Although everyone follows the route of nature, individual temperaments and talents vary, resulting in deviations of excess and deficiency. The sage takes the path people ought to take and regulates it, thereby becoming an exemplary for all under heaven. This is called "education", which encompasses rites, music, punishment, and the administration of societies. People are aware that they possess human nature but often do not realize that it originates from Heaven. They understand that there is a Way to follow but may not recognize that it stems from human nature. They know that the sage embodies instruction but may not see that in regulating himself, he aligns with what we all inherently possess. When scholars grasp this, they will naturally dedicate themselves to their studies and cannot help but do so. Therefore, Zisi begins by elucidating this point, which readers should deeply comprehend and silently acknowledge.*

The budget is a mechanism for resource allocation. The amount and mode of collection and expenditure depend not only on the type and scope of public policies and services that the government may offer, but also on the budget system and its capacity. The Way of budgeting is the basis and integral component of governance.

Note: The paragraphs marked with an asterisk (*) are sourced from Zhu Xi's *Sishu Zhangju Jizhu* (Collected Commentaries on the Four Books), specifically *Zhongyong Zhangju* (Commentaries on the Zhongyong), Chapter 1, pages 17–18.

Translator's Note: In this translation and the following chapters, passages from the *Zhongyong* (The Doctrine of the Mean) are marked as [Zhongyong], while Zhu Xi's commentaries are labeled [Commentary].

Y. Gou, *The Mean in Budgeting*, https://doi.org/10.1007/978-981-96-9592-8_1

What kind of philosophy, procedures, and norms should budgeting follow to effectively enable the government to perform its role and reduce financial risks? This is the fundamental question of the budget.

[Zhongyong] What is termed the Way cannot be deviated from for an instant. What can be deviated from is not the Way. Therefore, the Noble Man is cautious over what he cannot see, and vigilant in what he cannot hear.

[Commentary] The Way is the principle governing everyday affairs and the proper state of things. It manifests in use as the virtue of our original nature, embodied in the mind. Nothing exists without it, and it has always been present. Therefore, it is impossible to abandon it even for a moment. If it were possible to abandon it, we could not speak of following our nature. For this reason, the gentleman remains in constant awe. Though he neither sees nor hears it, he dares not neglect. Consequently, he adheres to the essence of the Heavenly principle and does not allow himself to stray from the Way even for a moment.*

The budget process is continuous, and the Way of budgeting remains constant. The budget demonstrates flexibility, adaptability, and responsiveness to the dynamic world. It sets a financial limit that regulates government behavior and controls fiscal risks. The Way of budgeting exists in any public policy and public service, whether it is for routine use or for trade-offs. It is all encompassing, and only by complying with it can budgeting be effective.

[Zhongyong] Nothing is more conspicuous than the concealed, and nothing is more evident than the subtle. Therefore, the Noble Man is careful when he is solitary.

[Commentary] "Concealed" means in the dark. "The subtle" denotes trivial things. Being "solitary" means being in a place where you alone are aware, while others are ignorant. In the dark, subtle things move, not leaving marks for other people to see, yet you alone clearly perceive the movement. Thus, nothing in the world is more evident than this movement. It is for this reason that the gentleman always harbors fear and exercises utmost caution. He thereby restrains human desires at the outset, preventing them from growing in secrecy and leading himself stray from the Way.*

The concealed aspects are often the essential aspects. The explicit budget, known and controllable, is the comprehensive, thorough, and all-encompassing budget management. The implicit budget, unknown and uncertain, is the part that cannot be directly addressed by the explicit budget.

In the initial stages of budget development, there is substantial space and freedom for the implicit budget, as there may not be adequate capacity to manage it effectively. In the advanced stages of budget development, there is still considerable space and freedom for the implicit budget, where the freedom is traded for responsibility. It motivates budget departments to enhance internal control, innovation, and creativity. Under what circumstances should the implicit budget be maintained? How much space should be reserved? What mechanisms should be employed to regulate and guide its operation? In an era where budgets increasingly stress planning, performance, and risk control, investigating these issues becomes a vital driver for budget improvement.

[Zhongyong] The mean is the state before joy, anger, sorrow and pleasure arise. When they arise in due measure, it is called harmony. The mean is the

great foundation of all under heaven. Harmony is the manifestation of the Way through all under heaven.

[Commentary] Joy, anger, sorrow and pleasure are all emotions. Before these emotions erupt, they are human nature without the slightest partiality, thus the state is termed "the mean". If they are properly expressed, then these emotions are also valid without going to extremes, thus it is a state of "harmony". The "great foundation" refers to the Heavenly mandated nature. All principles under heaven originate from it; it is the Way itself. The "manifestation of the Way" pertains to following our human nature. It is the source from which everything under heaven, past and present, collectively arises; it is the function of the Way. This passage underscores the virtue of human nature and emotions to illustrate that the Way cannot be abandoned.*

The mean and the harmony lie at heart of the Way of budgeting. The rules and processes of budgeting should reflect the spirit of the mean, stability and fairness. The outcomes and impacts of budgeting should indicate a state of harmony, effectiveness and coherence. The mean and the harmony are interrelated, as a stable and fair process is necessary for effective and balanced outcomes. The application of the mean in budgeting signifies the pursuit of harmony, and attaining a state of harmony is crucial to manifest the importance of balance.

[Zhongyong] When the mean and harmony are actualized, Heaven and Earth will be in their proper positions; and the myriad things will be nourished.

[Commentary] "To actualize" is to accomplish. "The proper positions" means to be at ease in their places. "Will be nourished" is to fulfill their lives. By harboring vigilance and fear, one can achieve an equilibrium of extreme quiescence. As a consequence of maintaining this perfect balance, Heaven and Earth will be in their proper positions. When solitary, one is also careful and meticulous to the point where there are no deviations or errors in handling matters, thus accomplishing harmony, leading to the nourishing of all things. Perhaps Heaven, Earth and the myriad things are originally one with me. When my mind is aligned, the mind of Heaven and Earth becomes aligned. When my inner energy is free flowing, so is the energy of Heaven and Earth. Thus, the efficacy of this principle is such. These supreme cultivation practices, the abilities of sages, do not depend on something external, as the cultivation of the Way indeed resides within. This concerns the Way itself and its function. Though they differ in rest and activity, once the Way itself is established, function will begin to operate. Thus, they are not two separate matters. Consequently, they are spoken of together and linked to the ideas expressed in the preceding text.*

The mean and harmony are the objective of budgeting. When the budget conforms to the mean, resources will be utilized in the proper way, and the outcome will be smooth and auspicious. The mean and harmony are not innate. They often require repeated practice and exploration in various dimensions such as institutions, mechanisms, policies and processes in order to attain improvement of budget systems, enhance the budget capabilities, and ultimately improve governance effectiveness. Through these efforts, a prosperous and comprehensive state of continuous development can be attained in various endeavors.

[Commentary] The preceding text constitutes the first chapter. Zisi transmits the Confucian school's teachings, which serves as the basis of his discourse. First, he establishes that the origin of the Way is derived from Heaven and is unchanging, while its essence resides within oneself and must not be abandoned. Next, he stresses the importance of preserving and cultivating it and introspection. Last, he discusses the moral influence of achieving the state of sages. In conclusion, learners should reflect upon themselves and derive benefits from it, eliminating the selfishness aroused by external temptations and cultivating their inherent virtues. This embodies the essence of what Yang Shi (1053-1135, a disciple of Cheng Yi) referred to as the core of the entire work. According to Yang Shi, in the following ten chapters, Zisi cites the words of Confucius to continue discussing the meaning of this chapter.*

The purpose and mechanism of budgeting are the main questions. Budgeting principles shape the budgeting process, and the budgeting process influences the budget outcomes. If the budgeting process violates the principles and participants forget their original intentions, budgeting will diverge from its intended purpose. Budgeting reform is not only about superficial changes, but rather making budgeting truly function as budgeting: effectively managing risks, ensuring rational allocation of resources, and stimulating active and creative participation from all stakeholders.

Budgeting is a dynamic and evolving process that encompasses infinite information about nature, society, and history. Like the tip of an iceberg, budgeting rules and procedures can only define, and budgeting texts can only explain a limited portion of it. No one comprehends everything about budgeting, as many mysteries still remain unexplored, invisible, unconceived, and not pondered. Yet these mysteries have constant effects on the budgeting's direction and outcome, consciously or unconsciously.

On the surface, budgeting appears as a process of interaction between income and expenditures, and budgets as outcomes of trade-offs. Essentially, economic, social, and cultural realities serve as the foundation and determining factors for budgeting principles and development directions. The objective of budgeting is to allocate and utilize society's resources with more efficiency and reach into infinite scopes, providing boundless space for innovation and improvement. With numerous instances of errors and failures in budgeting, budget participants learn through experience to humbly acknowledge the limits of their rationality, examine the nature of reality, control the scope of risks, evaluate the impact of measures, and accept political constraints. Market failure does not automatically imply government efficiency, and success in the short run does not guarantee long-term rationality.

Performance serves as a guiding principle for change. If progress is difficult, recognizing temporary limitations and waiting patiently for the right moment may prove more productive. If improvement opportunities exist, it is crucial to acknowledge the difference between thinking and doing, work in accordance with the situations, and march steadily towards strategic objectives over time. Budgeting aspires to achieve not only immediate results but also a fair, reasonable, and dynamic mechanism towards sustainable development.

Chapter 2
The Changes in Budgeting

[Zhongyong] Zhongni (Confucius) said: "The Noble Man adheres to the mean; the petty man goes against it.

[Commentary] The person who adheres to the mean is not going to one side or the other, nor going to extremes of excess and deficiency. The universal principle is regarded as the Mandate of Heaven and the most profound. Only a true gentleman can comprehend and embody it, while a petty person violates it.*

Economic conditions, political requirements, international landscape, social trends, and environmental changes all impact and shape budgeting to varying degrees. Can income, debt, expenditure, and institutional systems remain in equilibrium and avoid excess or deficiency? It is challenging, as the temptations of real interests are strong, and the benefits of budgeting are uncertain. Making timely decisions in response to changing circumstances inevitably leads to variations in the budget; only occasionally can they coincide. By adhering to the Way of budgeting, weathering challenges and taking risks, one can navigate through uncertainty and steadily move towards success.

[Zhongyong] The Noble Man seeks the mean and adheres to it; the petty man seeks the mean but acts heedlessly."

[Commentary] Based on the commentary of Wang Su (a Confucian scholar in the Northern Wei Dynasty [386-534]), the latter half of the sentence should be understood as "the petty man goes against the mean and acts heedlessly", and Cheng Hao and Cheng Yi concur with his view. We adopt this perspective. The gentleman practices the mean is because they possess noble virtues and can accord with circumstances in finding the perfect balance. The petty man goes against the mean is because they harbor a petty mindset and is devoid of fear and restraint. The mean does not have a fixed form; Its existence accords with circumstances. It is a universal principle. The gentleman comprehends that the mean resides within himself, so he is cautious about what he does not see and apprehensive about what he does not hear

Note: The paragraphs marked with an asterisk (*) are sourced from Zhu Xi's *Sishu Zhangju Jizhu* (Collected Commentaries on the Four Books), specifically *Zhongyong Zhangju* (Commentaries on the Zhongyong), Chapter 2, pages 18–19.

Y. Gou, *The Mean in Budgeting*, https://doi.org/10.1007/978-981-96-9592-8_2

- and so always practices the mean. In contrast, the petty man fails to grasp this point and thus indulges his desires without any restraint.*

Moderate budgeting emerges from a correct comprehension of the Way of budgeting, which is derived from rational analysis and deep reflection on historical experiences. It also originates from adhering to the Way of budgeting, reverence for basic principles, and continuous analysis, judgment, and adjustment. Uncertainty is the inherent characteristic of ubiquitous budgeting. Only by being cautious all the time can one maintain a balanced position. Those who presume they comprehend the Way of budgeting and manipulate the budget often bring disastrous consequences as they easily forsake principles, breach procedures, modify standards, and surpass limits. It is challenging to persistently adhere to the Way of budgeting, as the temporary benefits of deviating often lead budgeters to disregard significant risks.

[Commentary] The preceding text constitutes the second chapter. In the subsequent ten chapters, the meaning of "the mean" is discussed to further explicate the essence of the first chapter. Although the texts may not be composed as a coherent narrative, the ideas in them really do form a continuous thread. About the shift of emphasis from "harmony" to "keeping to the constant" (in accordance with circumstances), Ziyou (a scholar in the Spring and Autumn Period, circa 770-476 BCE) stated, "When speaking from the perspective of temperament and emotions, the term is 'practicing the mean and harmony'; when speaking from the perspective of moral conduct, the term is 'practicing the mean and keeping to the constant'." In fact, the term "mean" in "practicing the mean and keeping to the constant" encompasses the meanings of both "mean" and harmony".*

Budgeting is determined by the government, the market, and individuals, any of whom can affect the revenue and expenditure of the budget. It mirrors the government's policy agenda, market mechanisms and individual responses. The budget is affected by interactions in various dimensions such as the economy, politics, technology, and social development. Changes in these dimensions can influence the direction and content of the budget.

Budgetary work should comprehend, reconcile, and advance changes, as the relative stability of the budget results from adapting to changes. Resource allocation and utilization efficiency are improved through fully mobilizing all positive factors in changes. Correctness of budgeting stems from the correct approach. That is, to meet the needs of the people in both the short and the long term, make decisions based on facts, coordinate and balance various interests, respect objective laws, and reconcile different demands. Otherwise, the budgeting will deviate from the right path, exceeding the financial capacity or missing development opportunities in order to balance revenues and expenditures.

Chapter 3
The Challenges of Budgeting

[Zhongyong] The Master said: "The mean is the highest virtue. Few are those who can maintain it for long."

[Commentary] Both excess and deficiency miss the point of balance, that's why the virtue of the mean is the supreme principle. However, this virtue is something that all individuals inherently possess. Initially, it is not difficult to implement the mean. But as the instruction of the world declines and people fail to put them into practice, it becomes rare for this virtue to be attained. This has been the case for a long time now. The *Analects* of Confucius does not contain records of anyone attaining this principle.*

The Way of budgeting is difficult to comprehend, and implementing it is even more difficult. People who practice it to success are seldom seen in reality. Most people either underperform or over-perform. Under a centralized system, one person's incompetence can cause significant waves. Under a democratic system, one person's wisdom can hardly prevail against the ignorance of the masses. It is often challenging to adhere to correctness in the long run. Some may obstinately pursue their own ways, while others simply follow the tide. People rarely transcend their immediate interests and find it difficult to learn from history's lessons. Hastily, they switch from one error to another, making it difficult to allocate talent appropriately and fully utilize resources' potential. It seems that everyone blames external factors while being unable to find the correct direction and path for themselves.

[Commentary] The preceding text constitutes the third chapter.*

Implementation of budgeting principles is challenging. Despite the continuous emergence of new concepts, deviations from fundamental principles are persistent. For example,

---

Note: The paragraphs marked with an asterisk (*) are sourced from Zhu Xi's *Sishu Zhangju Jizhu* (Collected Commentaries on the Four Books), specifically *Zhongyong Zhangju* (Commentaries on the Zhongyong), Chapter 3, page 19.

Y. Gou, *The Mean in Budgeting*, https://doi.org/10.1007/978-981-96-9592-8_3

Budgeting should be rule-based, where expenditure cannot be made without budgeting. However, in practice, there are loose constraints during implementation, frequent additional adjustments, distorted final accounts, and the squeezing of resources due to pressing real needs.

Budgeting should be comprehensive, with all fiscal funds being planned and prioritized based on real needs. Yet, in reality, departmental interests lead to fragmentation, with each entity prioritizing their own budgets, encroaching upon fiscal space and undermining allocation efficiency.

Budgeting should be unified, integrating planning and budgeting, with long-term performance guiding annual budget arrangements. In practice, however, planning and budgeting often operate separately, lacking essential budgeting foundations and necessary performance information, resulting in impracticality and a lack of direction. Additionally, capital budgeting is managed separately from recurrent budgeting, without necessary coordination mechanisms. This leads to a coexistence of excessive investment and insufficient maintenance.

Budgeting should be transparent, with budget information being made accessible to the public in an understandable manner. Yet, in reality, the disclosure of budget information is often limited, and lacks sufficient detail and necessary explanations. Budget transparency has not become an important channel for interaction between the government and the public, nor has it exerted necessary pressure on government governance.

Budgeting should strive for balance, effectively controlling fiscal risks. However, in practice, some local governments fail to prudently control expenditures during economic expansion periods, resulting in heavy debt burdens. Mechanisms for preventing and controlling fiscal risks have not been established, leaving government operations in a state of unsustainable illusory prosperity.

These fundamental principles represent the core of budgeting. By comprehending and addressing these issues, as well as adhering to the principles, budgeting can create conditions for performance-oriented development. Frequent deviations from these principles will inevitably lead to budgetary regression, causing repeated setbacks in similar areas.

Chapter 4
The Reality of Budgeting

[Zhongyong] The Master said: "The Way is not practiced, and I understand why. The clever surpass it and the dull fall short. The Way is not revealed, and I understand why. The virtuous surpass it and the unworthy fall short.

> [Commentary] The Way is the universal principle and is equivalent to the mean. The clever, the dull, the virtuous and the unworthy cannot attain the mean because of their distinct nature. The clever, being excessively knowing, deem the practice of the Way inconsequential. The dull, being ignorant, do not know how to implement the Way. These reasons explain why the Way is not practiced. The virtuous, in their excess, consider the knowledge of the Way inconsequential. The unworthy do not practice the Way and do not seek how to comprehend it. Thus, the Way is not revealed.*

Mismatches in budgets often occur because the finance department is focused on development, while other departments concentrate on securing financial resources. The finance department oversees all aspects of budgeting, including setting goals, making budgets, following certain procedures, allocating money, and organizing evaluations. Unfortunately, the finance department, fearing a loss of control, frequently issues policies that may not be well-received. Instead of concentrating on budgeting, they spend too much time instructing other departments on what to do and what not to do.

Other departments may accept their financial allocations, busy working without clear direction and showing little concern for the role of budgeting in management. As a consequence, the budgeting diverges from its Way, as the finance department loses focus on budgeting balance, risk control, and fund management, while other departments muddle along budgeting, performance, and cost control.

To return to the Way of budgeting, departments should take their responsibilities seriously. It is necessary to clarify the relationships involved in budgeting, such as

---

Note: The paragraphs marked with an asterisk (*) are sourced from Zhu Xi's *Sishu Zhangju Jizhu* (Collected Commentaries on the Four Books), specifically *Zhongyong Zhangju* (Commentaries on the Zhongyong), Chapter 4, page 19.

Y. Gou, *The Mean in Budgeting*, https://doi.org/10.1007/978-981-96-9592-8_4

development strategies, decision-making mechanisms, institutional arrangements, role positioning, expenditure standards, information infrastructure, revenue generation, and resource allocation. Only by establishing a solid foundation can we avoid unnecessary troubles and mistakes, and realize effective budget management.

[Zhongyong] People all drink and eat, but few truly appreciate the taste."

[Commentary] The Way cannot be abandoned. When people fail to examine themselves, it leads to errors of excess and deficiency.*

Budgeting is a crucial activity that involves both spending and requesting money. However, different departments may have different perspectives and motivations for budgeting. The budget department may view budgeting as a chance to obtain more funds and spend them liberally, regardless of the actual needs. This may result in losing sight of the true priorities and objectives. The finance department may view budgeting as a matter of matching revenues and expenditures, without grasping the underlying rationale and implications.

This may lead to various undesirable outcomes. For instance, the budget may be simply replicated from the previous year, without any adjustments or innovations. The issues that are on the top of the agenda of the leadership may be addressed hastily, despite all challenges. Each stakeholder may be satisfied when the situation is favorable, or each expenditure may be indiscriminately cut when the revenue drops. Excessive debt may incur when pursuing rapid growth.

Without a clear Way of budgeting, the budget may become a directionless and soulless document that merely follows the trends. It is important to remember that the government revenue is derived from the people and should be used for the people's benefit and oversight. However, some people may be indifferent to the budget, assuming that the authorities will handle everything. Some people may be self-interested and prioritize their own gains over the common good.

The mission of budgeting, however, is to allocate resources and create value. In the budgetary planning and decision-making process, the focus should be on identifying value; in the implementation and audit phase, the focus should be on achieving and measuring value. Budgeting should not be a pursuit of personal interests, but a driving force for the government to actively enhance the well-being of the people and to support, supplement, and stimulate personal efforts.

[Commentary] The preceding text constitutes the fourth chapter.*

Budgeting is a dynamic and complex process that requires constant adaptation and innovation. The traditional mode of budgeting is challenged by changing circumstances and new problems that demand new solutions. Various budgeting approaches have been developed, such as milestone budgeting, program budgeting, performance budgeting, plan-program-budgeting, target-based budgeting, and performance-based budgeting, among others. However, none of these approaches can provide a definitive and lasting answer to all budgeting issues. They emerge and fade away in the flux of budgeting activities.

To navigate the Way of budgeting with grace, one must not only achieve a comprehensive understanding but also implement it effectively and adapt to evolving trends.

However, in practice, budgeting actions are often taken without clear reasoning and collaboration, regardless of the consequences and the realities, with an emphasis on the formalities rather than the substantive changes. This leads to a situation where all the efforts are wasted and trapped in a prisoner's dilemma. The solution to this may lie in returning to the fundamental principles and mechanisms of budgeting and its related institutions, optimizing the governance systems, aligning the interest mechanisms, achieving a comprehensive mobilization, and stimulating the initiative and creativity of all the stakeholders.

Chapter 5
The Ideals of Budgeting

[Zhongyong] The Master said: "How unfortunate that the Way is not pursued."

[Commentary] The Way is not practiced simply because it is not revealed.*

Budgetary practices often face challenges from budget ideals, but these ideals provide the guidance and potential for the budget. It is only by adhering to budget ideals that optimal budgets can be achieved.

[Commentary] The preceding text constitutes the fifth chapter. This chapter builds on the previous one and examines why the Way is not being practiced, and introduces the idea found in the following chapter.*

Budget concepts are numerous and diverse, but they are worthless if they cannot be effectively applied to regulate revenue and expenditure, enhance resource allocation, and drive performance. A specific budget model may address a problem at a certain point, but it may lose its efficacy or even become detrimental over time.

For instance, milestone budgeting reinforces control, but it may also impose a restriction; program budgeting emphasizes efficiency, but it may also compromise effectiveness; planning-programming-budgeting stresses planning, but it may also exceed management capacity and hinder implementation; performance budgeting aims at results, but it may also pose challenges in measurement and application.

As a Chinese proverb states, "A wise man adapts to changes; a knowledgeable man acts according to circumstances." Budgeting must be flexible and adaptable to changes or even initiate them.

Note: The paragraphs marked with an asterisk (*) are sourced from Zhu Xi's *Sishu Zhangju Jizhu* (Collected Commentaries on the Four Books), specifically *Zhongyong Zhangju* (Commentaries on the Zhongyong), Chapter 5, pages 19–20.

Y. Gou, *The Mean in Budgeting*, https://doi.org/10.1007/978-981-96-9592-8_5

Chapter 6
The Balance in Budgeting

[Zhongyong] The Master said: "Emperor Shun possessed great wisdom. He liked to inquire of others and examine their remarks. He concealed others' faults and highlighted their virtues. He balanced extremes and fostered equilibrium for the common good. Thus, Shun was worthy of his name."

[Commentary] Shun was regarded as a great sage because he did not depend only on himself alone, but sought wisdom from others. He would scrutinize shallow ordinary speech and extract every benefit. Seeing that Shun would cover up faults and promote good deeds candid and upright, everyone was willing to inform him of good deeds. "Two extremes" refers to the extreme divergences in public opinion. Indeed, everything has its two extremes, just like the notions of small and large, thick and thin. In pursuing goodness, if one grasps both extremes to find the balance, and then implement, then one has done the utmost with prudence. This can only be achieved with careful decision-making, providing justification for the successful exercise of the Way, free from excess and deficiency.*

Budgeting encompasses a two-step process. The first step involves the creation of a diverse set of potential projects, followed by a stringent review process to identify those deserving of support, the establishment of objectives and evaluation indicators, as well as the formulation of implementation strategies and monitoring frameworks. The second step entails the execution of projects that are congruent with strategic objectives and financially feasible. The significance of planning in this context cannot be overstated; it is integral to the success of budgeting efforts. A comprehensive and well-conceived plan is imperative for efficacious implementation. This planning process necessitates continual refinement, attention to detail, and the incorporation of provisions for potential risks and uncertainties.

[Commentary] The preceding text constitutes the sixth chapter.*

Note: The paragraphs marked with an asterisk (*) are sourced from Zhu Xi's *Sishu Zhangju Jizhu* (Collected Commentaries on the Four Books), specifically *Zhongyong Zhangju* (Commentaries on the Zhongyong), Chapter 6, page 20.

Y. Gou, *The Mean in Budgeting*, https://doi.org/10.1007/978-981-96-9592-8_6

Budget performance hinges on good design, calculation, monitoring, and implementation. Reviewers of the project pool should carefully select the proposals that are truly worthy of attention from numerous candidate. Budget allocations should aim to minimize expenditure while maximizing the outcomes within the financial constraints. The most important issues are often reflected in the people's voice, and the solutions to these issues also originate from the people and serve their interests. The solid foundation for budgets is established from refinement, differentiation, and logical improvement.

Chapter 7
The Consistency in Budgeting

[Zhongyong] The Master said: "Everyone claims 'I am wise', but when they are driven or induced in snares and pits, they don't know how to evade them. Everyone claims 'I am wise', yet when they decide to practice the mean, they cannot maintain it for a full month."

> [Commentary] When one chooses to practice the mean, one needs to distinguish among various manifestations of the universal principles. The issue of "inquiring of others" and "applying the mean" was addressed in the previous chapter. A situation may arise where an individual is cognizant of potential dangers but lacks the knowledge to circumvent them. Similarly, there may be instances where an individual is capable of making judicious decisions but fails to maintain them consistently. In both scenarios, such an individual cannot be considered truly wise.*

Budgets are subject to uncertainty, as rapid changes in economic, political, military, and international contexts can divert the budget from its planned course. Favorable economic conditions often result in overly optimistic budget arrangements, especially with substantial increases in fixed expenditures. Once the economic situation deteriorates with income declining, while the expenditures continue to escalate, it becomes difficult to achieve a balanced budget.

To avoid the budget trap, one must maintain calmness during economic overheating and be proactive during economic slumps. It requires adherence to fundamental budget principles. Articulating the principles may be simple, but abiding by them is challenging. Evading problems leads to further evasion, and compromising leads to even more compromises. Tragedies recur throughout history, as those self-evident principles are disregarded amid economic, political, and other influences, only to be rediscovered and applied after suffering hardships.

Note: The paragraphs marked with an asterisk (*) are sourced from Zhu Xi's *Sishu Zhangju Jizhu* (Collected Commentaries on the Four Books), specifically *Zhongyong Zhangju* (Commentaries on the Zhongyong), Chapter 7, page 20.

Y. Gou, *The Mean in Budgeting*, https://doi.org/10.1007/978-981-96-9592-8_7

[Commentary] The preceding text constitutes the seventh chapter. It builds on the great wisdom of Shun presented in the preceding chapter, and explores the reasons for the Way being concealed, in order to lay the foundation for the subsequent chapter.*

The budgeting process is replete with trade-offs and potential pitfalls.

For instance, loosening economic controls at the macro level might invigorate the economy but also lead to substantial deficits. Conversely, similar actions at the micro level could improve performance yet give rise to behavioral anomalies.

Furthermore, a top-down budgetary preparation may provide guidance, but there is a tendency for plans to exceed budgetary capacities, reducing them to mere rhetoric. Emphasizing management and efficiency during implementation can result in the oversight of actual impacts. Allocating funds for specific objectives might consume excessive fiscal resources, thereby limiting flexibility. While promoting innovation and diversifying revenue streams may diminish market space and accrue financial risks.

In all these cases, the interplay between responsibility and power, incentives and constraints, the present and future, and between rules and freedom presents both opportunities and risks. Without progress, there is no development; without caution, there is no safety.

In times of economic upturn, budgets often become overly ambitious, marked by grand plans and impulsive promises. Incremental budgets, while resolving temporary conflicts and demands and adhering to budgetary norms, can mask underlying problems.

In times of economic stagnation, the fallacy of perpetual budget growth would be exposed, halting the expansion of programs. Investments become sunk costs without ongoing input, assets depreciate rapidly, and commitments to obligations become challenging to honor.

When long-standing conflicts surface collectively, budgetary rules often become lenient in the face of reality, leading to the consistent violation of restrictive targets focused only on symptoms rather than root causes. This results in substantial implicit liabilities and future costs, ultimately borne by the people.

The recurrence of such issues prompts the question of whether there is a lack of understanding in how to progress. Despite differing manifestations, these problems often lead to similar conclusions. Basic rules and common sense, though fundamental, are invaluable in governance. The challenge lies in the application of this knowledge. Failure to learn from past mistakes leads to the repetition of these scenarios, and the allocation and usage of public resources will remain suboptimal unless there is adherence to fundamental principles and common sense.

Chapter 8
The Principles of Budgeting

[Zhongyong] The Master said: "Yan Hui was the kind of person who mastered the mean in such a way that, achieving a certain goodness, he would adhere to it firmly and never lose it."

> [Commentary] Yan Hui, a disciple of Confucius, possesses a profound grasp of the mean. This deep understanding allows him to discern and uphold the mean with precision. Consequently, his actions are neither excessive nor deficient, thus illuminating the Way.*

Comprehensiveness and balance are the essential principles of budgeting. Temporary deviations during discretionary policy-making are also intended to restore this principle in the medium and long term. Budget participants should always comply with and strive to revert to this rule, in order to enhance their resilience and make rational choices.

> [Commentary] The preceding text constitutes the eighth chapter.*

The fundamental principles are indispensable for budgeting. Governance is deficient without comprehensiveness, and unviable without balance in revenue and expenditure. While the era may vary and the mission of budgeting may evolve, comprehensiveness and balance should always be sought after whether the goal is managing risks, enhancing performance, or executing plans.

Note: The paragraphs marked with an asterisk (*) are sourced from Zhu Xi's *Sishu Zhangju Jizhu* (Collected Commentaries on the Four Books), specifically *Zhongyong Zhangju* (Commentaries on the Zhongyong), Chapter 8, page 20.

Y. Gou, *The Mean in Budgeting*, https://doi.org/10.1007/978-981-96-9592-8_8

Chapter 9
The Justice in Budgeting

[Zhongyong] The Master said: "An entire kingdom can be governed, ranks and salary can be renounced, and a sharp sword can be braved; yet, attainment of the mean remains elusive."

[Commentary] "To be governed" signifies the attainment of peace and order. These three matters - wisdom, benevolence, and courage - are esteemed as the most arduous challenges in the world. However, they do not inherently align with the mean, for those possessing these virtues can accomplish them through their own endeavors. Yet, while practicing the mean does not entail the difficulties of the three acts, it demands a profound understanding of righteousness, sincerity, and benevolence. Only those free from selfish human desires can achieve this aim. The three acts appear difficult yet attainable, while the mean appears attainable yet actually difficult. This is why only a few people can truly realize the mean.*

Budget entails various conflicting interests. Overemphasizing one aspect can impair the others while attempting to address them all simultaneously can weaken the effect. Partially stressing certain concepts and principles may resolve some issues, but may also create unintended trade-offs. The budgeting process can be reduced to a mere formality.

Budgeting must adjust to changes in contexts and objectives. Budgets should always be in place even though the fund users change. Thus, everything about budgets should change, otherwise, today's successes could become tomorrow's challenges. Strictly following set doctrines and principles doesn't always yield desirable outcomes. It is vital to preserve a certain degree of flexibility, even necessary ambiguity, to enable future adaptations and innovations.

[Commentary] The preceding text constitutes the ninth chapter. It also builds on the preceding chapter and introduces the following chapter.*

Note: The paragraphs marked with an asterisk (*) are sourced from Zhu Xi's *Sishu Zhangju Jizhu* (Collected Commentaries on the Four Books), specifically *Zhongyong Zhangju* (Commentaries on the Zhongyong), Chapter 9, page 21.

Y. Gou, *The Mean in Budgeting*, https://doi.org/10.1007/978-981-96-9592-8_9

Budgeting ideals are fairness and rationality. This means that all aspects, from project justification to resource allocation, should be reasonable, with participants maintaining a composed and rational approach. Grandiose speeches and extreme, one-sided pursuits may seem attractive in the short term, but they often fail to sustain long-term performance.

Opportunistic approaches to budgeting might temporarily secure excess funds, yet these methods, lacking in producing desired outcomes, can damage the credibility and future funding capabilities of the budget department. Employing a carrot-and-stick strategy to balance diverse budgetary demands may be effective initially. However, if it fails to tackle the underlying critical issues, this approach will lead to greater compensatory requirements in the future.

Budget reforms, while impactful at the outset, require ongoing, comprehensive, and coordinated efforts to avoid stagnation. Effective budgeting is not about going for publicity, ticking a box, or just getting by. It involves a pragmatic approach that seeks truth from facts, aiming to create a lasting impact.

There are times when the budgetary department must acknowledge its inherent limitations, as ambitious goals can be thwarted by current challenging conditions. It is prudent to remain cautious of lofty, unrealistic ideals, as their pursuit can be counterproductive. Instead, a focus on feasible and foundational improvements is a vital component of the budgetary process, ensuring steady progress towards achieving budgetary ideals.

Chapter 10
The Strength of Budgeting

[Zhongyong] Zilu inquired about strength.

[Commentary] Zilu, also known as Zhongyou, is a disciple of Confucius. Esteeming strength, Zilu inquired about its nature.*

Ambitious leadership tends to favor aggressive budgets. However, without sound budgeting, it is hard to realize ambitions. The challenge of budgeting is not merely about managing large revenues and expenditures in the short term, but rather ensuring that long-term obligations are met.

[Zhongyong] The Master said: "Are you referring to the strength characteristic of the South, that of the North, or the strength by your own standard?

Budget demands, patterns, and measures vary according to regional, temporal, cultural, and traditional differences. There is no universal optimal approach to budgeting but rather a context-specific one. When conducting budgeting, it is essential to adjust to local circumstances and refrain from applying solutions that are incompatible with the environment.

[Zhongyong] Being broadminded and gentle in teaching and refraining from punishing wrongdoing hastily is the strength of the South. The Noble Man follows this.

[Commentary] "Being broadminded and gentle in teaching" indicates the virtue of being tolerant and lenient in instructing others who may fall short. "Refraining from punishing wrongdoing hastily" implies the capacity to withstand adversity without retaliating. The Southern culture, characterized by gentleness and flexibility, esteems the ability to overcome others through patience and forbearance as a mark of strength, embodying the Way of the gentleman.*

Note: The paragraphs marked with an asterisk (*) are sourced from Zhu Xi's *Sishu Zhangju Jizhu* (Collected Commentaries on the Four Books), specifically *Zhongyong Zhangju* (Commentaries on the Zhongyong), Chapter 10, page 21.

Y. Gou, *The Mean in Budgeting*, https://doi.org/10.1007/978-981-96-9592-8_10

Stability fosters moderation in budgeting. During tranquil periods, there is a propensity to seek optimization within existing frameworks and to alleviate budgetary conflicts by acknowledging reality and making marginal adaptations. This can be accomplished either by reaching a compromise that appeases all stakeholders and keeps the budgetary conflicts within tolerable limits or by deferring decisions and allowing time to settle budgetary conflicts.

[Zhongyong] Being armed with weapons and armor and die without fear - this is the strength of the North. The forceful possess it.

[Commentary] The Northern culture is renowned for its resilience, valuing boldness and strength as the key to surpassing others. This is the way of the strong.*

Grand epochs engender grand budgets. Budgets during times of transition tend to concentrate on tackling major issues, whether it be inducing major alterations in budget magnitude or configuration, or effecting radical changes in budget allocation mechanisms and modes. Major transformations in the budgetary domain often correspond to the needs of the contemporary undergoing change.

[Zhongyong] The Noble Man exhibits harmony without following blindly. What true strength this is! He maintains balance without bias. What true strength this is! He is steadfast in supporting the Way when it prevails in the land. What true strength this is! He remains loyal to the Way even when it perishes in the land. What true strength this is!"

[Commentary] These four virtues are what you ought to consider strength. When the Way prevails in the land, he makes no changes to what he held dear before. When the Way does not prevail in the land, he makes no changes to what he has held dear throughout his life. This is what is meant by "practicing the mean may be unattainable". Those who do not transcend their personal desires are incapable of choosing to practice the mean and holding to it. What could be greater than the strength of the noble person! The Master spoke to Zilu in this manner so to restrain his impulsiveness and promote in him moral courage.*

Budgeting should be approached with the dual objectives of achieving stability and fostering initiative. Stability, in this context, is not synonymous with rigidity; rather, it entails the establishment of a flexible framework characterized by equitable and optimally allocated resources and organizational structures. Within this framework, policies and projects are informed by the current situation and adapted to changing circumstances. Initiative, on the other hand, should not be misconstrued as mere restlessness. Rather, it involves the pursuit of budgetary equilibrium and sustainable development within clearly defined objectives and viable strategic frameworks.

The essence of the Way of budgeting is not merely about balance and stability, nor is it exclusively about prosperous development. It is about confronting challenges courageously, weighing all aspects, and cultivating a budget system and ecosystem that is both stable and effective.

[Commentary] The preceding text constitutes the tenth chapter.*

Budgets serve diverse purposes, leading to variations in their structure and objectives. When budgets are crafted with a primary focus on procedural adherence, governmental operations can proceed smoothly within established parameters, minimizing internal conflicts. This approach ensures the fulfillment of fundamental societal needs and facilitates progress across various domains.

Alternatively, when budgets are designed to align with the visionary goals of specific leadership, a comprehensive reevaluation of values occurs. This entails envisioning ambitious schemes, prioritizing major strategies and projects, and reallocating resources without undue constraint from cost–benefit considerations or adversity-induced constraints.

A people-centric budgeting approach seeks to align with public sentiment while avoiding pandering to vulgarity, judiciously determining resource allocation based on pragmatic assessments, and upholding commitments to citizenry.

It becomes evident that the philosophical underpinnings of budgeting favor the latter approach. To instantiate a people-centric budget, it becomes imperative to align fiscal plans with societal aspirations, recognizing the need to adapt in times of crisis and adversity, fostering a culture of vigilance and self-improvement, and striking a balance between regulatory control and performance optimization.

Chapter 11
The Common Sense of Budgeting

[Zhongyong] The Master said: "Those who pursue esoteric ideas and behave eccentrically will be recounted by future generations—this I will not do.

"Pursuing esoteric ideas and behaving eccentrically" refers to probing into abstruse principles and taking abnormal behavior excessively. Doing so may deceive the world and garner undeserved recognition, leading future generations to praise such a person. This behavior exemplifies excessive knowledge without choosing the good and overstepping in practice without adhering to the mean. It is a display of strength where one ought not to be strong. How could the Sage possibly engage in such actions?*

A budget should not be cosmetic, transforming only in form. Innovative approaches and drastic measures may garner support transiently, but they often fall short of long-term effectiveness.

[Zhongyong] Some individuals pursue the Way and abandon it halfway—this I will not do.

"To pursue the Way" means to be capable of choosing the good. "To abandon it halfway" suggests a lack of strength. Therefore, despite possessing the requisite wisdom to progress along this path, one's conduct may fall short of the ideal due to a failure to fully harness inner strength. The sage, therefore, does not dare to cease without effort, for sincerity knows no end; naturally, he is incapable of stopping.*

Budget ideals cannot be achieved overnight; they take time. Political changes can lead to budget changes, and changes such as economic shocks and the international environment can affect budgets, which often cannot be implemented exactly as planned, and realistic needs often override careful design. Reforms such as performance budgeting and zero-based budgeting have come and gone, and none of them have solved all budget problems once and for all, but it is also after many budget troubles that budget capacity has improved.

Note: The paragraphs marked with an asterisk (*) are sourced from Zhu Xi's *Sishu Zhangju Jizhu* (Collected Commentaries on the Four Books), specifically *Zhongyong Zhangju* (Commentaries on the Zhongyong), Chapter 11, pages 21–22.

Y. Gou, *The Mean in Budgeting*, https://doi.org/10.1007/978-981-96-9592-8_11

[Zhongyong] Some individuals adhere strictly to the mean, withdrawing from worldly affairs and remaining unknown to others, yet harbor no sense of regret for their chosen path. Only a sage can do this."

[Commentary] Not "pursuing esoteric ideas and behaving eccentrically", he adheres to the mean. Being incapable of "abandoning halfway", he "withdraws from the worldly affairs and remains unknown to others, yet harbors no sense of regret". This is the virtue of the mean, epitomizing the pinnacle of wisdom and benevolence. Courage is not required here and yet all is well. Confucius himself exemplified this ideal but abstained from assuming the title of sage, thus, he says, "Only a sage is capable of this."*

The purpose of budgeting resides in the control of financial risks, the allocation of funds in accordance with established standards, and the enhancement of the institutional framework and capacity for governance. Given the changing circumstances and the accompanying challenges, the stability and efficacy of the budgetary framework hinge upon institutional robustness. Consequently, the efficacy of government initiatives need not necessarily align with budgets, but with the ability of budgetary stakeholders to leverage prevailing circumstances to effectuate meaningful change, thereby optimizing the functionality of the budgetary mechanism.

[Commentary] The preceding text constitutes the eleventh chapter. Zisi's quotation of Confucius serves to elucidate the profound significance of the first chapter. This foundational text expounds upon the virtues of wisdom, benevolence, and courage as the entry to the Way. It is for this reason that chapters open with illustrations from the Great Shun, Yan Yuan, and Zilu, who represents wisdom, benevolence, and courage respectively. Lacking any one of these three you cannot cultivate the Way and fully realize virtue. For further elaboration, subsequent analysis is provided in Chapter 20.*

The Way of budgeting is common sense. The budget serves as a crucial framework and foundation, enabling the fiscal sector to comprehend, articulate, and fulfill its objectives. Conforming to old habits, or seeking expediency, is often a result of the neglect of common sense. Adherence to budgetary fidelity involves a steadfast commitment to common sense. This entails a consistent respect for people's will and laws governing social development. Additionally, it is imperative to continuously uphold and implement the fundamental budgetary principles of comprehensiveness and balance across various dimensions, including institutional frameworks, mechanisms, processes, and standards.

Chapter 12
The Rationality in Budgeting

[Zhongyong] the Way of the Noble Man is extensive in its reach, yet remains subtle.

[Commentary] The application of the Way is extensive. Its essence is subtle.*

The Way of budgeting is extensive and subtle. The budget encompasses not only broad outlines but also meticulous details. It plays a pivotal role in assisting the government to orchestrate fiscal inflows and outflows essential for national governance. The figures presented in the budget report represent an epitome of the entire fiscal picture. Thus, a comprehensive understanding of the budget necessitates a fundamental grasp of government operations. This principle holds equally true for the processes of reform and oversight within the budgetary context.

[Zhongyong] Average men and women, even if ignorant, know something of the Way; yet in its ultimate form, even the sage cannot know. Average men and women, despite their limitations, can practice it to some extent; yet in its ultimate form, even the sage cannot carry into practice. As great as the universe is, people still have dissatisfaction. When the Noble Man refers to its greatness, he implies its incomprehensibility due to its immense scope. When he speaks of its smallness, he means an irreducible essence.

[Commentary] The Way of the gentleman begins close at hand, within the relationships within the family and household, and extends far, encompassing matters beyond even the reach of sages and the heavens and earth. It is so vast that nothing lies outside of it, and so minute that nothing lies within it. This can be considered "extensive". However, the principle that makes the Way of the gentleman so is obscure and difficult to discover. What can be known and achieved is but one aspect of the Way. Even at the highest level, sages may not fully understand or attain it. This means that even sages have limitations in comprehending the entirety. Hou Guo (1077-1147) said: "There are things that sages do not know, such as Confucius asking about rituals and governance. There are things they cannot accomplish, such as Confucius

Note: The paragraphs marked with an asterisk (*) are sourced from Zhu Xi's *Sishu Zhangju Jizhu* (Collected Commentaries on the Four Books), specifically *Zhongyong Zhangju* (Commentaries on the Zhongyong), Chapter 12, pages 22–23.

Y. Gou, *The Mean in Budgeting*, https://doi.org/10.1007/978-981-96-9592-8_12

> not holding office, and Yao and Shun worrying about widespread implementation." I believe that people feel regret towards Heaven and Earth, such as the partiality in covering, bearing, transforming, and nurturing, as well as the abnormal phenomena in calamities and disasters.*

While the budget report is accessible and superficially comprehensible to all, the rationale behind its specific allocation of income, expenditures, and debt remains complex.

The finance sector and the budget sector each have their own perspectives, which may differ from the viewpoints of the government's decision-makers. This diversity of opinions means that no single entity has a comprehensive understanding of the entire budgetary process.

At its core, budget execution involves the collection of taxes and the disbursement of funds in accordance with established rules and plans. However, the strategies for effective tax collection and the optimal use of funds to achieve desired outcomes are constantly evolving questions.

The field of budgeting boasts a lengthy history, yet there remains significant scope for further exploration and understanding in both its theory and application. This exploration encompasses broad macroeconomic issues such as medium-term budget planning, the scale of finances and debt, and the overall fiscal system, all of which are subjects of extensive debate.

Simultaneously, there is a nascent inquiry into more microeconomic aspects, including the standards for expenditure quotas and the setting and measurement of performance objectives. These areas represent the forefront of current budgetary research and practice.

[Zhongyong] *Shijing* (The Book of Songs) says: "The hawk flies high in the sky; the fish dances in the deep." This signifies that height and depth are both discernible.

> [Commentary] This excerpt is drawn from the "Foot of Mount Han" section of the chapter of "Major Odes" of *The Book of Songs*. Zisi referenced this poem to exemplify the evident transformations and nurturing of all things, which are the workings of this principle, referred to as "extensive". However, the underlying reason for this is not something that can be perceived by the senses, thus it is termed "subtle". Therefore, the Masters Cheng said: "This section is the key point that Zisi wants to convey to people. It is vivid and lively, and readers should ponder it deeply."*

The budgetary framework is inherently event-driven, adapting dynamically to evolving trends and temporal shifts. It is essential to ensure that necessary allocations are adequately secured to realize intended outcomes.

For example, areas identified for reduction should be decisively curtailed to enhance overall performance. Aspects requiring standardization must be homogenized to preclude disorder. Likewise, elements that can benefit from liberalization should be freed to foster vitality.

While the superficial aspects of the budget exhibit a multitude of changes, at a deeper, more substantive level, there exists a harmonious diversity within the various components. This dichotomy between the apparent anomaly on the surface and the underlying coherent diversity is a fundamental characteristic of effective budget management.

[Zhongyong] The Way of the Noble Man originates with the people, yet in its ultimate form, it transcends to a universal application.

[Commentary] This statement encapsulates the essence of the preceding discussion.*

The fluctuations in the budget present as highly specific and seemingly devoid of any universal principles. Yet, akin to a colossal tree that originates from a diminutive seedling, there often lies an underlying principle within even the most minute financial transactions. The inability to discern the evolving patterns in fiscal inflows and outflows can lead to marginal errors or substantial divergences, resulting in awkward or incomplete financial outcomes, or a disequilibrium between income and expenditure.

[Commentary] The preceding text constitutes the twelfth chapter. The discourse of Zisi serves to reaffirm the central tenet articulated in the initial chapter: the Way cannot be abandoned. In the subsequent eight chapters, the teachings of Confucius are invoked through a diverse array of quotations.*

The concept of budgeting is fundamentally rooted in logical reasoning. It necessitates that the sector requesting funds elucidates the reasons for their financial needs, while the sector responsible for budgetary decision-making explains the rationale behind monetary allocations. Additionally, any adjustments made during the implementation phase should also be clearly justified.

Effective communication requires tailoring the message to suit different audiences. This involves articulating the rationale in a clear and simple manner for the general public, providing in-depth explanations to experts, and also presenting an overarching summary to decision-makers.

By adapting the depth and complexity of the information to the needs of each audience, the message can be superficial or in-depth, overt or subtle, direct or indirect, explicit or implicit. A clear explanation means being unequivocal about the reasons for action or inaction and the timing of these decisions. A budget, fundamentally, is a forward-looking plan for fund allocation.

It poses questions such as: What are the intended actions? How much funding will be required? What outcomes are anticipated? These considerations are essentially theoretical hypotheses and directives that are yet to materialize and should be progressively implemented and tested throughout the budgetary process.

Given the uncertainty brought about by various visible and hidden factors affecting the budget, achieving the desired budget rationality requires a continuous effort to understand and apply the laws governing the development of various factors amidst changes.

This involves deepening the understanding and awareness of basic facts and concurrently improving mechanisms for budget planning, decision-making, implementation, and evaluation. Only through such an approach can participants in the budgeting process achieve the desired level of rationality in their budgetary endeavors.

Chapter 13
Budgeting with People in Mind

[Zhongyong] The Master said: "The Way is not distant from man. If you practice a Way that is distant from man, this cannot be the Way.

> [Commentary] The Way is to conform to one's nature, an aspect both comprehensible and actionable by individuals. Consequently, it often manifests in interactions that are not remote from one's experiences. If one claims to follow the Way, yet despises the humble and near as inadequate, and instead seeks to accomplish lofty and distant endeavors, then this is not the Way. *

The budget is, ultimately, about people, with its efficacy contingent upon societal evaluation. Any budget that diverge from the present and future necessities of the people goes contrary to the principles of sound budgeting. Regardless of whether the budgetary process is top-down or bottom-up, it is essential that it originates from and ultimately serves the public interest.

The efficacy of the budget is largely determined by its equity and practicality. Effective budgetary performance management relies on clearly defined performance goals and the formulation of evaluation metrics.

A thorough comprehension of genuine needs, management foundations, technical capabilities, and external circumstances forms the cornerstone of the budgetary process. In essence, the budgeting process integrates considerations from the past, present, and future.

[Zhongyong] *The Book of Songs* says: 'Cutting a branch for an axe-handle, you have an immediate model.' When you flip an axe-handle to cut a branch for another, looking with a squinted eye at the handle, you may still think that the model is too far to follow. Thus, the Noble Man govern people in line with their nature, and help them to mend their ways until they succeed.

Note: The paragraphs marked with an asterisk (*) are sourced from Zhu Xi's *Sishu Zhangju Jizhu* (Collected Commentaries on the Four Books), specifically *Zhongyong Zhangju* (Commentaries on the Zhongyong), Chapter 13, pages 23–24.

Y. Gou, *The Mean in Budgeting*, https://doi.org/10.1007/978-981-96-9592-8_13

[Commentary] This excerpt is drawn from the "Carving Axe-handles" section within the chapter of the "Songs at Bin" of *The Book of Songs*. It is said that when a person uses an axe to cut wood to make an axe handle, the dimensions and form of the new axe handle are already present in the existing handle. Yet, there remain subtle differences, making the task seem distant to the woodcutter. Similarly, in the governance of people, the principles of human conduct are inherently present within those being governed, with no true disparity among them. Thus, the governance of a gentleman lies in applying these individuals' inherent principles back onto themselves. If the individual can rectify themselves, governance ceases and is not further imposed. This approach entails requiring individuals to act based on what they can comprehend and practice, rather than demanding they transcend the common populace to follow the Way. As Master Zhang Zai (1020-1077) wisely stated: "When you expect from people what the common people expect, it is easy for them to comply." This is indeed correct. *

The budgetary process does not represent a mere intersection of past and present; rather, it allows for contemporary considerations to draw upon historical arrangements. However, given the dynamic nature of circumstances and social development, these traditional arrangements may not always align seamlessly with new realities. Therefore, it is imperative to engage in thoughtful deliberation and seek solutions that address the evolving needs of the people.

The concept of a definitive, unalterable budget is a fallacy. In reality, the budget is perpetually subject to change, reflecting the fluidity of various socio-economic factors. Solutions that are deemed acceptable within the budgetary framework are consistently in flux. This variability is attributable to changes either in the demographic of beneficiaries or in the financial landscape, characterized by shifts in income and expenditure.

[Zhongyong] Loyalty and reciprocity are not far from the Way. Never do to others what you would not do to yourselves.

[Commentary] To fulfill one's own heart is loyalty; extending one's heart to others is reciprocity. Hence, avoiding imposing on others what you yourself do not desire is an act of loyalty and reciprocity. Measuring others' hearts by one's own heart has always been consistent, revealing that the Way is never distant from the people. Therefore, the principle of not imposing on others what you do not wish for yourself is a practice of the Way that remains close to the people. As Master Zhang Zai wisely stated: "To love others with the heart that loves oneself is to be truly benevolent." This is indeed correct. *

A budget, in its ideal form, serves the collective interest. It embodies the principles of social justice, ensuring that the needs and interests of all stakeholders are considered and balanced. Attaining a state of tranquility and contentment within the budgetary process is contingent upon this equitable approach. Favoring the interests of one party to the detriment of another can precipitate disputes and undermine stability.

[Zhongyong] The Way of the Noble Man embraces four virtues, yet I have not fully attained any one of them: I fail to do what a son should do to his father; I fail to do what a minister should do to his ruler; I fail to do what a younger brother should do to his elder brother; I fail to do what a friend should first do to another. In the practice of ordinary virtues, in being cautious in normal speech, if he falls short, the Noble Man dares not but strive harder; if he has

any excess, he dares not carry on to the end. In speaking, he aligns with his actions, and in actions, he aligns with his speech. How can the Noble Man fail to be sincere?".

[Commentary] The Way is never distant from people. To hold others accountable, one must first hold oneself accountable, thus engaging in self-cultivation. When one's virtue is insufficient, one should encourage oneself and strive harder in practice. When one's words are excessive, speaking less brings one closer to the pinnacle of caution. When caution reaches its peak, words will align with actions. When actions are diligently carried out, they will align with words. This describes the noble person's conduct - how can it not be sincere? This is a testament to their virtue. All these are efforts to practice the Way without distancing oneself from people. As Master Zhang said: "Using the heart that holds others accountable to hold oneself accountable, the Way is present everywhere." *

The process of budget integration presents significant challenges. It often occurs that the planning and execution phases of the budget are handled by different entities. Discrepancies frequently arise between budgetary needs and the approvals granted.

Furthermore, the allocation of funds, the timing of government procurement, and the budgetary schedule may not align effectively. Additionally, there is often a divergence between prescribed income and expenditure standards and the actual fiscal requirements. A disconnect between budget management and asset management is also commonplace. These factors collectively contribute to a disjointed budget and suboptimal performance.

To address these issues, a two-tiered approach is necessary. At the macro level, there is a need to transform government functions, reinforce the primary responsibility of budget management, and establish a more coherent relationship between authority and responsibility.

On the micro level, it is imperative to undertake a comprehensive review and optimization of business processes. This involves a commitment to realism and the pursuit of excellence, solidifying the underpinnings of budget management, and fostering a culture that is conducive to effective budgeting practices.

[Commentary] The preceding text constitutes the thirteenth chapter. The Way is not distant from people. What ordinary people can achieve surpasses even the reach of Confucius. The limitation of saints in this regard is attributed to the extensive manifestation of the Way. This constraint is inherently linked to the concept of subtlety. The subsequent chapter delves further into these themes. *

The budget fundamentally serves the people, with individuals constituting both its primary objective and its most dynamic component. The preparation, decision-making, and execution of the budget are human-driven processes, with the ultimate merit of these processes being gauged by their utility to people. Therefore, it is critical not to focus solely on the monetary aspects of the budget, overlooking the human element.

Effective budgeting necessitates a comprehensive appreciation and consideration of the human factor. This involves establishing a balanced relationship between individuals and their interests, while also fostering their motivation and creativity.

It also involves understanding and stimulating human potential, setting ambitious targets and striving to maximize performance within the constraints of available resources. Besides, it is imperative to acknowledge and accommodate human limitations. This encompasses ongoing monitoring and adjustment of performance objectives throughout the budgetary process, timely modification of relevant strategies, and minimization of unnecessary risks.

Finally, it is advisable to maintain flexibility in institutional arrangements, allowing for innovation and evolution. A tolerant attitude towards the inevitable cycles of revision, spontaneous ideas, and potential failures is crucial, as these elements can be fertile ground for significant advancements in budgetary performance.

Chapter 14
Within Budget

[Zhongyong] The Noble Man acts in accordance with his station and does not covet what lies beyond it.

[Commentary] They fulfill their duties based on the responsibilities of their current position, without harboring desires for what lies beyond. *

While the budget addresses certain issues, it does not provide a panacea for all problems. The process of budgetary preparation involves the collection and integration of budgetary requirements. The decision-making process associated with the budget determines the allocation of resources, with the economic climate, societal realities, and the proficiency of governmental management influencing the outcomes of revenue and expenditure.

The concept of a budget is often nebulous, frequently bearing expectations that extend beyond its inherent scope. The determinants of a budget's success or failure should be sought outside conventional parameters, rendering it unproductive to restrict oneself to the confines of the budget in search of answers.

[Zhongyong] When he is in a position of fame and fortune, he acts from the positon of fame and fortune. When in poverty and humbleness, he acts within from the positon of poverty and humbleness. When dwelling with uncultured tribes, he acts from the positon of uncultured tribes. When in stress and difficulty, he acts from the positon of stress and difficulty. The Noble Man never fails to content himself with the situation he is in.

[Commentary] This means to act in accordance with one's position. *

Failing to capitalize on favorable economic conditions results in missed developmental opportunities; conversely, indiscriminate expansion during unfavorable

---

Note: The paragraphs marked with an asterisk (*) are sourced from Zhu Xi's *Sishu Zhangju Jizhu* (Collected Commentaries on the Four Books), specifically *Zhongyong Zhangju* (Commentaries on the Zhongyong), Chapter 14, page 24.

Y. Gou, *The Mean in Budgeting*, https://doi.org/10.1007/978-981-96-9592-8_14

periods imposes a significant burden. Budgetary strategies differ between highly developed and underdeveloped regions.

Prosperity and poverty, ease and adversity, are all facets of a single domain. By focusing on necessary actions, one can attain tranquility and harmony, while neglecting this principle invites unending harm.

In periods of prosperity, the rapid pace of economic growth often obscures underlying financial risks. Infrastructure projects and promises may provide temporary satisfaction and attract attention, but they often leave behind prolonged periods of hardship and crisis.

Adversity, however, can be constructive: during financial difficulties, adherence to fundamental principles, structural adjustments, foundation strengthening, and enduring the pressures of transformation and the pains of reform can lead to long-term stability and performance.

Budgets are dynamic, adapting to changing circumstances, and there is no universal budgetary model that should be applied indiscriminately.

[Zhongyong] When in a higher position, he does not despise those below. When in a lower position, he does not court the favor of those above. He rights himself but does not demand perfection of others, thus harboring no resentments. He blames neither Heaven above nor men below.

[Commentary] This section signifies that a gentleman does not aspire to undertake tasks beyond his responsibilities in his current position. *

The budget is underpinned by philosophies, regulations, institutions, and standards, with a substantial proportion of budgetary interactions striving to transcend these constraints. The pursuit of local interest may result in a substantial loss of global interest or increased efficiency of resource allocation.

Budgetary regulations, institutions, and standards frequently serve as the inception point for budgetary interactions. This initial point is pivotal, as it largely dictates the transactional costs and the overarching trajectory of the interaction process. The figures presented in the budget report merely represent the outcome of the budgetary process; the essence of the budget is fundamentally shaped by the practical application of these underpinnings.

[Zhongyong] The Noble Man remains adaptable amidst change and anticipates his destiny. In contrast, the petty man resorts to perilous practices and relies on fortuity.

[Commentary] "To remain adaptable amidst change" is to act according to one's position. "To anticipate one's destiny" implies not wanting to undertake tasks beyond his responsibilities in his current position. "Fortuity" refers to obtaining what one does not rightfully deserve. *

For the sustainability of a budget, it is imperative to harmonize strategic business planning with the available budgetary capacity. A budgetary crisis can emanate from an unregulated navigation through intricate phenomena, an inflated rate of progress incongruous with reality, or an unwavering preoccupation with past events.

[Zhongyong] The Master said: "The act of practicing archery is akin to cultivating oneself as a Noble Man. Upon failing to hit the target, one should seek the cause within oneself."

[Commentary] The rationale behind Zisi's citation of Confucius' words was to provide a conclusive remark to the preceding discourse. *

Budget failures are attributable to numerous factors, including resource misallocation, control failure, or the accumulation of risk. However, the root causes lie in the disregard or incorrect application of the foundational concepts and principles of budgeting.

The crucial strategy for circumventing or addressing budgetary crises involves a profound contemplation of the basic budgetary concepts and principles, followed by rectification of the root causes.

[Commentary] The preceding text constitutes the fourteenth chapter. The discourse presented herein comprises the words of Zisi. Sentences that do not commence with the phrase "The Master said" are all attributed to Zisi. *

Budgets ought to be customized to align with the prevailing circumstances. The notion of a perfect budget is a myth; the most effective budget is one that fulfills the requisite needs.

In periods of financial abundance, the budget should proactively identify and cater to societal needs, adjust the tax burden, optimize the expenditure structure, and strive towards ambitious goals.

In periods of financial hardships, the budget should exploit potential income sources, stringently regulate entitlement expenditures, and curtail operational costs to navigate the harsh reality.

When conditions are favorable, the budget serves as a fulcrum to enhance distribution and incentive mechanisms, thereby fostering comprehensive performance improvement.

Under unfavorable conditions, the budget functions as a tool to standardize foundational elements, thereby enhancing the internal control mechanism and mitigating financial risks through standardized preparation and diligent implementation.

Each period is characterized by a distinct budgetary theme; identifying the accurate theme enables proficient execution. Imitating others, blindly following trends without considering the context, and adopting foreign concepts with the aim of drastically changing one's fate often lead to counterproductive results and reduced efficiency.

At various stages, different budgeting methodologies are selected to address practical issues, such as zero-based budgets, target budgets, and performance budgets. Even within the same performance budget, the utilization of performance information varies across countries, regions, and time periods. Actions should be undertaken when necessary and halted when appropriate.

Practice is the sole criterion for verifying the truth. If a budget reform measure fails to yield noticeable effects, the cause can only be unearthed from the current budgetary practice.

Furthermore, the persistent evaluation dilemma of budget performance management can only be resolved by adopting a broader perspective of the budget cycle, which is instrumental in effecting a fundamental change in the situation of addressing the issue of setting objectives and indicators at the preparation stage.

Chapter 15
Collaboration in Budgeting

[Zhongyong] The Way of the Noble Man can be compared to traveling: To go far, one must start from a nearby point. It can be compared to climbing: To go high, one must start from a lower position.

[Commentary] "To be compared to" means to be likened to. *

The attainment of budgetary objectives is not an instantaneous process. The foundation of budgeting performance lies in a standardized budgetary procedure, rational expenditure benchmarks, and a robust implementation mechanism.

For example, the underpinning of the medium-term budget comprises a situation analysis, a visionary plan, and a forecast of revenues and expenditures. The efficacy of budgeting in government procurement relies heavily on a mature market, coupled with a well-established culture of contract management.

The successful execution of a reform concept necessitates not only the fostering of innovative approaches and the development of new capabilities, but also the effective resolution of historical issues of diverse magnitudes. Naturally, significant transformations require time and persistence. A deficit of patience and determination, combined with a tendency to follow fleeting trends, will invariably result in unfulfilled objectives.

[Zhongyong] ***The Book of Songs*** **says: "The peaceful union of husband and wife is like zither and lute in tune. When siblings all get along, the harmony is entrancing. Therefore, cultivate a wholesome household and derive pleasure from your spouse and offspring."**

[Commentary] This statement is an excerpt from the section of "Chinese Bush Cherry" within the "Minor Odes" chapter of *The Book of Songs*. *

Note: The paragraphs marked with an asterisk (*) are sourced from Zhu Xi's *Sishu Zhangju Jizhu* (Collected Commentaries on the Four Books), specifically *Zhongyong Zhangju* (Commentaries on the Zhongyong), Chapter 15, page 25.

Y. Gou, *The Mean in Budgeting*, https://doi.org/10.1007/978-981-96-9592-8_15

The budget necessitates a state of harmony. Initially, this harmony manifests in the form of diversity, wherein the logic underpinning budget planning can vary (often significantly), yet the disparate interests are more or less actualized during the budgetary process, thereby establishing a degree of equilibrium among them.

The budget also necessitates a state of cooperation, characterized by the budgetary process culminating not in incessant conflict and division, but in the recognition of disparate interests and values. From a societal perspective, the budget represents a cooperative process and a mechanism for improvement, facilitating the allocation of social resources in a manner that optimizes societal benefit via the government budget.

[Zhongyong] The Master said: "Our parents will feel at ease."

[Commentary] Confucius recited the verse and lauded it, asserting that if a man can foster harmony with his spouse and extend the same courtesy to his siblings, it would bring tranquility and contentment to his parents. Zisi cited the verse and articulated these words to elucidate that no matter how distant your goal is, you must start from where you are, and to climb high one must begin from the bottom. *

The budget also necessitates a state of ease. First, we have to create channels to facilitate communication of the public. Next, we need to achieves equilibrium by identify a widely accepted solution.

The fundamental value of the budget lies in the collective interests of the people, which serves as the primary benchmark for evaluating the validity and feasibility of various budgetary strategies and techniques.

[Commentary] The preceding text constitutes the fifteenth chapter. *

The budget represents a long-term collaborative endeavor, involving both intragovernmental and extra-governmental entities. By consulting iteratively during the budget process, stakeholders can pinpoint their missions and role boundaries, get resource allocation finalized, and establish a collaboration mechanism based on the government's objectives and tasks.

Given the intricate and comprehensive nature of governmental work, it is often challenging to coordinate and integrate the various functionalities of the government in the implementation of the budget. It necessitates an effective synergy mechanism, a long-standing tradition of cooperation, and a public spirit dedicated to the pursuit of excellence.

Undoubtedly, the budget is not a self-serving mechanism within the government. Interactions between the government and the private sector, social organizations, and the people are pivotal. On the one hand, the introduction of non-governmental organizations can engender new opportunities for diversification and enhanced performance. On the other, the participation of these sectors can enrich the budget and significantly augment its accuracy, transparency, and effectiveness.

These efforts may incur higher consultation costs and require greater budgetary capacity, thus posing more uncertainties and risks to the government. However, they also serve as drivers of transformation in the governance structure and ability. By addressing these challenges, the government enhances its comprehension of and rapport with enterprises, non-governmental organizations, and the people. Therefore, these efforts contribute to the improvement of the governance eco-system and its performance.

Chapter 16
Beyond Budgeting

[Zhongyong] The Master said: "The merits of ghosts and gods are truly amazing!

[Commentary] The Masters Cheng said, "Ghosts and gods are manifestations of the functions of Heaven and Earth, and they symbolize creation." Master Zhang Zai stated, "Ghosts and gods are the products of *yin* and *yang*." From the perspective of the *qi*, ghosts are considered the spirits of *yin*, and gods are the spirits of *yang*. In the context of a single *qi*, the expanding entity is deemed a god, and the contracting entity is considered a ghost, signifying one being. "Merits" refers to the functions.*

The budget exerts a substantial influence on economic and social progression, as well as the standard of living of the people. Therefore, the magnitude of the budget impacts the interplay between the government and the market, thereby affecting the efficiency and vitality of the economy. On the one hand, the budget structure influences the prioritization of public investments and determines the state of national construction, public services, and social welfare. On the other, the budgetary mechanism serves as a crucial incentive and regulatory mechanism for public affairs, influencing the mindset and conduct of public officials.

[Zhongyong] In the quest to perceive them, they remain elusive to the sight. In the attempt to discern them, they remain inaudible. There is no entity that they do not encompass.

[Commentary] Ghosts and gods lack tangible form or audible sound, yet there is no aspect of the beginning or end that is not engendered by the convergence and divergence of *yin* and *yang*. Thus ghosts and gods are manifested as physical substance. There is no entity that they do not encompass. This relation aligns with what *Yijing* (The Book of Changes) says about the hexagrams and their explanations.*

Note: The paragraphs marked with an asterisk (*) are sourced from Zhu Xi's *Sishu Zhangju Jizhu* (Collected Commentaries on the Four Books), specifically *Zhongyong Zhangju* (Commentaries on the Zhongyong), Chapter 16, pages 25–26.

Y. Gou, *The Mean in Budgeting*, https://doi.org/10.1007/978-981-96-9592-8_16

The budget is ubiquitous. It functions to administer the nation, manage administrative services, regulate business operations, and oversee the daily necessities of individuals, encompassing food, attire, accommodation, and transportation.

[Zhongyong] These ghosts and gods compel the people of the world to fast for purification, and wear elegant clothes in order to participate at the sacrifices. They are overflowing, seeming to be above, seeming to be on the left, and on the right.

[Commentary] The ability to evoke awe, reverence, and admiration, and to manifest so conspicuously, serves as evidence of their physical substance and their all-encompassing nature. Confucius said "The *qi* that rises up to the sky is called the bright and clear, the burning and withering, and the sorrowful and mournful. This is the essence of all things, and the manifestation of the deities." His remark conveys a similar meaning.*

Budgets warrant serious consideration. The budget being implemented constitutes a responsibility that necessitates adherence in a standardized and efficient manner. The budget to be proposed is a plan to be executed within the confines of one's capabilities and to the best of one's abilities. The execution of a predetermined budget is subject to uncertain internal and external influences, while an uncertain budget proposal is predicated on a relatively fixed budgetary foundation. On the surface, the budget adheres to established rules, yet the underlying influences would surface from time to time.

[Zhongyong] *The Book of Songs* says, 'The approaches of the deities are beyond our understanding. How could we possibly treat them with indifference?'

[Commentary] This statement is an excerpt from the section of "Prudent Look" within the chapter of "Major Odes" of *The Book of Songs*.*

The inherent uncertainty within the budget dictates that it be both robust and steady. Given the uncertainties present in the economic landscape, both international and domestic environments, and public affairs, it is imperative for the budget to establish an appropriate crisis response mechanism.

As the world becomes increasingly "chaotic", the complexity of budgeting escalates. The larger the uncertainty within and beyond the public domain, the more room there is for budgetary adjustments. However, an increase in the scope for budgetary adjustments correspondingly amplifies the challenge of budgetary control. Consequently, budgetary capacity must be equipped to confront uncertainty and risk.

[Zhongyong] Thus, the subtle becomes manifest. Thus, the outpourings of sincerity cannot be suppressed."

[Commentary] Indeed, sincerity is the true and unfeigned. The union and separation of *yin* and *yang* are all real. Therefore, its manifestation cannot be repressed."*

In the context of the allocation and utilization of government funds, the budget must acknowledge the prevailing circumstances, identify effective utilization strategies, and undergo objective evaluation. This constitutes a cyclical process that encompasses not only the entire public sector but also the broader society associated with the provision of public goods and services, extending its influence to organizations and individuals in foreign countries.

A sound budgetary system inspires pragmatism, trust, collaboration, and creativity. This is the essence of a sustainable budget: it must reflect reality, respect human nature, and encourage goodwill and innovation.

[Commentary] The preceding text constitutes the sixteenth chapter. The state of being imperceptible and inaudible can be characterized as subtlety. The act of encompassing all aspects is deemed extensiveness. The initial three chapters are about the smallness of extensiveness. The subsequent three chapters, conversely, are about the scope of extensiveness. The current chapter interplays between the concepts of extensiveness and subtlety, and the notions of greatness and smallness.*

The interplay of economic conditions, political interests, societal atmosphere, cultural norms, international affairs, and unpredictable occurrences collectively shape the trajectory and substance of the budget. Discerning which elements will exert dominance over the budget is a complex task; seemingly rational justifications may prove futile, ostensibly absurd outcomes may have sound reasoning, and the factors that remain unseen and unheard often truly dictate the eventual outcome.

The budget cannot be approached lightly, as alterations can emerge at any given moment, in any location, presenting either opportunities or formidable challenges. Consequently, seasoned budget practitioners have no alternative but to exercise caution and respect. The notion of sound sleep is an unrealistic expectation. It resembles an unending sequence of exhaustive chess matches, prompting questions about income and expenditure, gainers and losers.

As long as the government persists, the budget will continue to evolve according to its inherent logic. While we undoubtedly possess substantial knowledge about budgetary laws, the complexity of the budget is a reflection of the intricacies of nature, society, and human nature, and the expanse of unexplored territory remains vast.

Chapter 17
The Essence of Budgeting

[Zhongyong] The Master said: "Shun was indeed a filial son. His virtue was that of a sage. He was revered as an emperor. His wealth was all-encompassing, extending to everything within the four seas. He offered sacrifices in the ancestral temple, and his sons and grandsons continued these sacrifices in his honor.

[Commentary] In this context, the reference to sons and grandsons pertains to the descendants of Shun, namely Yu Si and Duke Hu of the State of Chen.*

A budget's success depends on both its conceptual and practical aspects. It requires not only a clear and precise budgetary concept, supported by appropriate institutions, procedures, and work flows, but also a budgetary outcome that achieves broad consensus, which is the core of the budgetary dilemma. Different viewpoints may generate incompatible concepts, and conflicting interests may produce adverse practices. The history of budgeting is marked by various budgetary models, none of which can offer a universal solution for all problems.

[Zhongyong] Thus, it can be said that those of great virtue inevitably attain their rightful position, receive their due reward, gain their deserved recognition, and enjoy longevity.

[Commentary] Shun lived to the age of 110.*

A successful budget requires a sound concept as its foundation. Budget norms, process optimization, and technology upgrade may be important, but without a budgetary principle that can adjust to changing circumstances, the budget often turns into a mere formality with reduced effectiveness.

[Zhongyong] When Heaven gives birth to all things, it cultivates each entity in accordance with its potential. Consequently, Heaven nurtures the burgeoning sprout and topples the leaning tree.

Note: The paragraphs marked with an asterisk (*) are sourced from Zhu Xi's *Sishu Zhangju Jizhu* (Collected Commentaries on the Four Books), specifically *Zhongyong Zhangju* (Commentaries on the Zhongyong), Chapter 17, page 26.

Y. Gou, *The Mean in Budgeting*, https://doi.org/10.1007/978-981-96-9592-8_17

[Commentary] "To nurture" means *qi* comes and accumulates; "To topple" means *qi* disperses and disappears.*

Budgets are influenced by the dynamics of things. They are evaluated based on performance and outcomes, but also by their long-term implications, allocating resources to areas with growth potential and divesting from areas that ought to be discontinued.

The execution of a budget transforms potentialities into realities, and a budget should envision potentialities, assess these potentialities, and make decisions within a constrained temporal framework. Budgets represent imperfect choices, yet the choices made within a budget should aspire towards perfection.

[Zhongyong] *The Book of Songs* says: 'The Noble Man performs the joyful rites, displaying his splendid virtues. He benefits his people and the officials; he receives blessings from Heaven; he is protected and ordained by Heaven, and Heaven bestows upon him a mandate.'

[Commentary] This passage is an excerpt from the section of "Ceremonial Music" within the chapter of "Major Odes" of *The Book of Songs*.*

The budget is inherently a public entity. The interests of the people serve as both the genesis and the evaluative criterion of the budget. The enhancement of the budgetary capacity, including planning, execution, monitoring and assessment, is contingent upon a deepened comprehension of the public's interests and an improved capability to actualize these interests.

[Zhongyong] Hence, individuals of profound virtue inevitably receive the Mandate of Heaven."

[Commentary] The one who receives the Mandate of Heaven assumes the role of the Son of Heaven.*

The budget is not self-determining. It can only fulfill its intended function when the appropriate governance and development concepts are effectively implemented.

[Commentary] The preceding text constitutes the seventeenth chapter. This chapter commences with the application of the Way in daily activities, and extends it to its utmost, revealing the extensive applicability of the Way. The underlying reason for this extensive applicability lies in the influence of subtlety. This interpretation is further echoed in the subsequent two chapters.*

The primary objective of a budget is to optimize the distribution of resources. The budget aims to allocate funds to individuals and initiatives that will enhance performance. When the allocation aligns with the intended objectives, the budget is deemed accurate, and theoretically, all budgetary efforts should be directed towards exploration and adaptation in this regard.

Initially, errors can occur, and what appears to be effective may not always yield the desired results. The pertinent question is whether these errors can be prevented from persisting. Adjustments or suspensions during implementation, or an alternative plan for the forthcoming year, may be necessary.

Errors may still remain despite these measures, either because of the absence of a superior option, or because of the influence of minority interests over the majority, or the other way around. Imbalanced interests undermine the foundation of beneficiaries and resources, regardless of their size, which leads to resources abandoning unproductive projects and pursuing new opportunities and paths.

When opportunities arise, projects with potential receive funding and are executed, which may result in performance. Performance, whether hidden or visible, is not always promptly recognized, fully understood, and acknowledged. If performance is not clear and convincing, the budget may be withdrawn, and the project may be terminated.

The budget is essentially about public investment, which, when accurately invested and effectively executed, yields performance. Performance represents the interests of the people. The budget should identify the interests of the people, concentrate on these interests, and consider the realistic and long-term interests of the people, while steadfastly upholding these interests.

While it is true that the budget is a game, the true test of victory or defeat is whether it serves the interests of the people. When optimal allocation and effective implementation are achieved from this standpoint, then budgetary performance is realized.

Chapter 18
The Budget Cycle

[Zhongyong] The Master said: "The only one who didn't suffer from grief was King Wen, given that his father was King Jili and his son was King Wu. His father established his foundation, and his son continued his practices.

[Commentary] This passage pertains to the deeds of King Wen. *Shangshu* (The Book of History) says that "King Jili was diligent in serving the royal house," indicating that his actions were also accumulating merit and benevolence.*

The budget ought to be devised within a medium- to long-term framework. Significant transformations necessitate sustained endeavors to optimize the tax base, restructure expenditures, enhance the fiscal system, and manage fiscal risks, all with a long-term perspective. Present budgetary challenges may originate from a previous decision, while current decisions frequently exert influence on the future for an extended duration. Therefore, it is crucial to exercise discretion in budgetary matters.

[Zhongyong] King Wu simply carried forward the great cause started by the Great King, King Jili, and King Wen. Upon donning his armor, he took control of the whole realm and he never failed to live up to the great reputation the people accorded to him. He was revered as a king. His wealth was all-encompassing, extending to everything within the four seas. He offered sacrifices in the ancestral temple, and his sons and grandsons continued these sacrifices in his honor.

[Commentary] This narrative pertains to King Wu of Zhou. The Great King, referred to as the father of Jili, laid the groundwork for the king's career, as per *The Book of History*. As stated in *The Book of Songs*, "The Great King established the foundation amidst the downfall of the Shang Dynasty." King Wu wore the armor to vanquish King Zhou of the Shang Dynasty.*

Significant transformations in the budget frequently stem from a process of long-term accumulation. The budget management system reform in 2000 aimed to address

Note: The paragraphs marked with an asterisk (*) are sourced from Zhu Xi's *Sishu Zhangju Jizhu* (Collected Commentaries on the Four Books), specifically *Zhongyong Zhangju* (Commentaries on the Zhongyong), Chapter 18, pages 26–27.

Y. Gou, *The Mean in Budgeting*, https://doi.org/10.1007/978-981-96-9592-8_18

the rapid revenue growth and the reduced fiscal discipline that resulted from the reform and opening up, especially the tax sharing system reform in 1994.

The full implementation of budget performance management reform in 2018 and the further budget management system reform in 2021 are necessary measures for the new stage of national development, considering the swift improvement of the level of basic budget management and the worsening situation of revenue and expenditure.

With regard to medium-term expenditure planning, which intermittently surfaces and recedes in budget management, it has made multiple appearances and retreated discreetly, but it has never truly departed. Planning is an indispensable requirement of the budget, and the dilemmas of today will serve as valuable experiences for tomorrow.

[Zhongyong] King Wu was bestowed with the Mandate of Heaven in the later stages of his life. The Duke of Zhou completed the great cause initiated by King Wen and King Wu. He conferred kingly titles to his great grandfather and his grandfather, offered sacrifices to former princes with the royal ceremonial rites, and disseminated this ceremony to all nobles, ministers, officers, and the general people. If the father held the position of a minister and the son served as a scholar-official, then the burial would be conducted for a minister and the sacrifices would be made for a scholar-official. Conversely, if the father was a scholar-official and the son was a minister, then the burial would be conducted for a scholar-official and the sacrifices would be made for a minister. The mourning period of one year applied to the ministers, whereas the three-year mourning period was applicable up to the king. In the mourning for parents, there was no differentiation based on social class."

> [Commentary] This passage pertains to the Duke of Zhou. The posthumous conferment of the title of king upon the Great King and King Jili was an estimated intention of King Wen and King Wu of Zhou to trace the origin of the empire. The term "former princes" refers to all ancestral generations from Danfu's father, Zu Gan, up to the first ancestor, Hou Ji. Sacrifices were offered to the former princes with the ceremonial rites befitting a king, thereby honoring the providence of the Great King and King Jili. The rites were established and propagated throughout the world, ensuring that the ranks of the deceased were utilized for burials, the ranks of the living were utilized for sacrifices. The mourning period of less than one year was exempted for the vassals, and reduced for scholar-officials. Funerals of parents were conducted uniformly, irrespective of social status. The rites began with oneself and were extended to others.*

The Budget Law serves as a mirror to budgetary realities and provides an exposition of budgetary ideals. The law was initially promulgated in 1995, underwent revisions in 2015, and saw the issuance of implementing regulations in 2020.

The primary focus of the Budget Law is the regulation of management and the fortification of control. It provides clear and precise guidelines on how to prepare the budget, implement decisions, execute the budget, evaluate and audit, and control financial risks.

Familiarity with the Budget Law facilitates a comprehensive understanding of budget responsibility, the budget process, and other related practices. However, the scope of the budget extends beyond this, with the law merely touching upon aspects such as budget performance, budget disclosure, budget participation, and the medium-term budget. This is primarily due to the fact that the practice is not sufficiently deep and thorough, and there is a lack of mature experience and consensus.

While budget control is essentially in place, there is a pressing need to deepen departmental internal control and urgently strengthen performance management and medium-term plans. This is an objective reflection of the Budget Law on the reality of budgeting.

[Commentary] The preceding text constitutes the eighteenth chapter.*

Budgets are perpetually in motion and have no definitive endpoint. Multiple budget cycles operate concurrently, with one wave cresting before the next, and participants transitioning between different budgetary timescales. There is no such thing as a purely current budget; present revenues and expenditures may be influenced by decisions made in the distant past, and forthcoming revenue and expenditure choices will significantly impact future budgets.

Budgets are baseline instruments, which embody the cumulative outcomes of previous achievements, negotiations, and trade-offs. They are also rational onstructs, which mirror the spirit of the times, with different themes in different periods. Inevitably, budgets adapt to the changing needs of the times through income and expenditure adjustments.

In the long term, the annual budget is merely an artificially demarcated period, and the general budget items can span a few years, several decades, or even generations. The short-term effect does not encapsulate the long-term impact, making it challenging to measure budget performance.

Changing the budget is no simple task; hence, without clear advantages, solid arguments, and incentives, there is no point to engage in the substantial work. Moreover, even if a long period has passed and performance is inadequate, interest groups may still concentrate on a small amount of self-interest.

"Life is endless from generation to generation; the river and the moon maintain a consistent appearance year after year." Often, despite meticulous planning and strenuous struggle, the budget remains unchanged. Change necessitates robust leadership, appropriate political directions, favorable economic conditions, and unforeseen opportunities. But is change invariably beneficial?

If there are no micro-foundations and long-term plans for dramatic change, but only passing trends or political imperatives, little will be achieved other than keeping participants occupied and accumulating financial risk.

To prevent self-imposed changes, avoid impulsive actions, and ensure that the budget system is dynamic, high-performing, and sustainable, the government must exercise self-restraint and self-motivation, and adhere to some fundamental budget rules: controlling the size of the budget, managing revenues and expenditures, elaborating and disclosing the budget, controlling the size of the debt, implementing budget responsibility and enhancing performance, etc.

These rules are the product of past experience, rational judgment, and trade-offs. They will restrict the government's budgetary behavior and motivate the government to act proactively on the budget, while simultaneously guiding the reasonable expectations of participants.

Compliance with these rules necessitates a gradual modernization of the governance system and capacity, as well as a proper balance between the government's current and long-term budgetary arrangements in the face of economic hardship and political pressure.

Chapter 19
The Traditions of Budgeting

[Zhongyong] The Master said: "How completely King Wu and the Duke of Zhou actualized their filial piety!

[Commentary] The discussion in the subsequent chapter regarding the filial piety of King Wu of Zhou and the Duke of Zhou aligns with the universal interpretation of filial piety. This is also what Mencius referred to as "being respectful".*

The budget serves as a harmonization of divergent interests, striking a balance between the realities and the budgeting ideals. It is crucial to safeguard operations, uphold priorities, and maintain fiscal equilibrium. Concurrently, it is equally important to execute the collective will of the people and embody the underlying philosophy and ethos of governance throughout the process.

[Zhongyong] Through the practice of filial piety, they faithfully followed their ancestors' wishes and fulfilled their deeds.

[Commentary] The preceding chapter indicates that King Wu succeeded Great King, King Jili, and King Wen in their endeavors, thereby gaining dominion over the world. The Duke of Zhou completed the great cause started by King Wen and King Wu to his forefathers. This practice embodies the continuation of the aspirations of predecessors and the narration of significant state affairs. The subsequent text discusses this in the context of the sacrificial rites that he established, which are applicable to both the senior and the junior alike.*

The budget is fundamentally people-centric. The needs of the people evolve in response to various changes, and correspondingly, the budget adapts; as societal progression occurs, the people would demand a commensurate improvement in budgetary capacity. The ideal of budget allocation is to accomplish substantial tasks with minimal expenditure; the objective of budget execution is to maximize output and generate positive outcomes with reduced spending.

Note: The paragraphs marked with an asterisk (*) are sourced from Zhu Xi's *Sishu Zhangju Jizhu* (Collected Commentaries on the Four Books), specifically *Zhongyong Zhangju* (Commentaries on the Zhongyong), Chapter 19, pages 27–28.

Y. Gou, *The Mean in Budgeting*, https://doi.org/10.1007/978-981-96-9592-8_19

[Zhongyong] During the spring and autumn, they cleansed the ancestral temple, laid out the sacrificial vessels, displayed the ceremonial outfits, and prepared the seasonal foods.

[Commentary] In reference to the ancestral temple: there were seven sacrificial vessels for the Son of Heaven, five for the feudal lords, three for the ministers, two for the scholar-officials, and one for the Official Teacher. These vessels represent the collected treasures of preceding generations, such as the red knife, jade artifacts, the river map of the Zhou Dynasty, among others. The ceremonial outfits, inherited from the ancestors, were worn during the sacrifice. Each of the four seasons is associated with distinct foodstuffs, such as lamb, pig, meat, paste, incense, and the like, which are typically presented in spring.*

To comprehend the budget, it is crucial to grasp the fundamental concepts, ideas, and principles, while also acknowledging the specific systems, processes, and standards. It is equally important to appreciate the intricate interplay of changes and constants within the budget.

Frequently, it is only after navigating through a series of complexities that one realizes the true essence of a particular budgetary principle. Often, it is through the seemingly monotonous repetition of daily tasks that we come to understand that the ostensibly simple process underlying the original is, in fact, not simple.

[Zhongyong] The sacrificial rites in the ancestral temple serve to arrange the order of the senior and junior branches of the family. The ranks of nobility are used to distinguish the noble and the humble. The merits of service are used to distinguish the worthy and the unworthy. By having the junior offer the toast to the senior, they kept the junior involved. By hair color, they distinguished seniority.

[Commentary] The order within the temple was determined according to the ancestral lineages. When a sacrifice was conducted in the temple, all sons and brothers were present in this order. The ranks were categorized into dukes, marquises, ministers, and scholar-officials. The ritual of honoring the senior entailed the sons of the guests and brothers each raising a goblet to honor the elders with wine, followed by drinking with each other. The act of honoring something in the temple also involved the junior, who were to offer the toast to the senior. Upon the completion of the sacrifice and the commencement of the banquet, the color of hair was used to distinguish between the elders and the young for the seating arrangement.*

A budget needs to be well-structured. The forecast of revenue and expenditure, coupled with the utmost effort and the capacity to fulfill needs, determines the reasonable scale of debt. The ratio of operational expenditure and capital investment elucidates the balance between government operation and development. The division of the fiscal system ascertains the degree of centralization and decentralization, while the adjustment of expenditure standards either constricts or expands the limited fiscal space.

This vast and intricate system is a rational construct, embodying innumerable ideals and objectives. It is also the outcome of habit and compromise, constrained by limited funds, information, capacity, and time. Fulfilling the budget is acceptable, but achieving satisfaction is preferable.

[Zhongyong] To take the positions of their forefathers, to carry out their rituals, to performed their music, to revere those whom they respected, to love those who were dear to them, to serve the deceased as though they were living, and to serve the departed as though they were still with us: this is filial piety to its utmost level.

[Commentary] Those who are esteemed and cherished include the ancestors, forefathers, descendants, and commoners of the late king. Upon their passing, they were termed deceased; following their interment, they were referred to as departed. Both appellations denote the former sovereigns. This marks the conclusion of the preceding two sections, which both expound upon the fulfillment of their ancestors' aspirations.*

The budgetary system operates on a foundation of authorization, characterized by stringent regulations at virtually every juncture. For example, tuition fees, after being remitted to the treasury, could become a revenue item. Once approved, expenditure budgets are subject to rigorous enforcement, with additional adjustments typically prohibited.

The treasury stipulates varying approval requirements for payments, contingent on the nature and scale of the expenditure. Any expenditure surplus not utilized within a two-year period is retracted. Debt issuance is regulated through quota control, necessitating local governments to secure authorization prior to incurring debt.

This system presents a dichotomy: on one side, there are immutable rules, while on the other, there exists a requirement for the rapid, efficient, and unrestricted utilization of funds amidst a complex and dynamic environment. The call for deregulation is akin to a wave surging towards the embankment of regulation. When obstructed, it engenders an even larger wave. The enduring impact of this dynamic will either lead to the destruction of the embankment or instigate the formation of new rules, thereby redefining the relationship between the wave and the embankment.

[Zhongyong] The suburban sacrifices are offered to worship the Supreme Deity, while the rites at the ancestral temple are conducted to honor the ancestors. One who can perform both suburban sacrifices and ancestral rites is capable of governing the realm with the ease of pointing to one's own palm."

[Commentary] The winter sacrifice means offering sacrifices to Heaven; the summer sacrifice means offering sacrifices to Earth. Great sacrificial rituals are carried out by the king, or "Son of Heaven", in honor of his ancestors. These sacrifices are performed throughout the year, exemplifying the continuity of ritual observance. The rites must be grounded in reason. The analogy of pointing to the palm of the hand illustrates the ease with which these principles can be discerned. This bears a notable resemblance to the teachings of the *Analects*, albeit with variations in length due to differing versions.*

Budgets necessitate a realistic approach, addressing the most pressing and tangible needs, while simultaneously upholding tradition and maintaining consistency in fulfilling past commitments. In reality, however, problems are everywhere, and there are many places where money needs to be spent.

Past commitments accrue annually, consuming half or more of the budget. Unresolved issues are frequently deferred to the future, resulting in recurring deficits and accumulating debts. Eventually, a juncture is reached where the narrative cannot persist, necessitating a choice between mandatory expenditures and discretionary expenditures. Consequently, some commitments, which were once deemed indispensable, are either forsaken or adjusted to accommodate new spending.

Budgeting should address urgent needs while honoring commitments. The fundamental principle is to strike a balance between these two requirements.

[Commentary] The preceding text constitutes the nineteenth chapter.*

The budget builds upon the past, exhibiting continuity and progress. As public services escalate annually, an increasing proportion of the budget is allocated to routine expenditure. This becomes ingrained over time, perpetually raising the level of coverage, the minimum wage, and social security, thereby exerting substantial pressure on budget balance. If revenue growth is constrained, this trend could encroach upon the limited fiscal space, rendering the budget inert and captive to past decisions.

The government must balance the budget, be prudent, and strive to better serve the people. This means constantly improving resource allocation. A future-oriented budget inevitably involves a process of continuous improvement: seeking initial public opinion, identifying budgetary needs, gathering further public input, reviewing the budget, and optimizing both existing resources and new allocations.

Past expenditures should not be used as a justification for their continuation in the future. We should scrutinize past expenditures with the same rigor as we assess new expenditures, revisit the history of these expenditures, and analyze their strengths, limitations, and potentials from historical experiences. Their validity and feasibility for the future should be evaluated on whether their objectives, plans, standards, costs, methods, and effects align with the needs of the people and whether there are better options available.

Being budget-aware suggests the need to enhance fiscal responsibility, procedures, systems, and capacity. To achieve this, we should evaluate and monitor the budget cycle, communicate to the public, assess all expenditures, align the budget with performance, eliminate inefficiencies, and improve effectiveness. This way, the budget can strengthen itself, optimize resources, and enable the government to be more innovative, vibrant, and responsive to the people's real needs.

Chapter 20
The Budget System

[Zhongyong] The Duke of Ai inquired about governance.

[Commentary] The Duke of Ai, sovereign of the Lu State, bore the name Jiang.*

The budget inherently possesses a political character, demonstrating a high degree of sensitivity to political dynamics. Ultimately, alterations in the political landscape will be manifested through modifications in the budget.

[Zhongyong] The Master said: "The governance of King Wen and King Wu is inscribed on the ancient tablets. When they had the right people, the government thrived, and when they didn't have the right people, the government faltered.

[Commentary] It is the king and his officials who determine the course of governance.*

The Budget Law, along with various associated laws and regulations, represent relatively stable and constant elements within the budget. The more explicit and specific these regulations are, the more standardized and transparent the budget becomes, albeit at the expense of a diminished capacity to implement discretionary policy.

Participants in the budget are the most dynamic variables within it; the higher the mobility of these participants, the greater the uncertainty of the budget. Alterations in key budget actors often serve as the primary catalyst for budgetary changes. Such change can either foster development or precipitate chaos and unrest.

[Zhongyong] When the people are right, the government prospers; when the ground is right, plants thrive. The administrations of King Wen and King Wu flourished like fast-growing weeds.

[Commentary] Having the right people in a government is analogous to the planting of a tree in fertile soil, which grows fast. Bushes and reeds, which readily mature into living

---

Note: The paragraphs marked with an asterisk (*) are sourced from Zhu Xi's *Sishu Zhangju Jizhu* (*Collected Commentaries on the Four Books*), specifically *Zhongyong Zhangju* (*Commentaries on the Zhongyong*), Chapter 20, pages 28–32.

Y. Gou, *The Mean in Budgeting*, https://doi.org/10.1007/978-981-96-9592-8_20

plants, experience particularly rapid growth. This underscores the ease with which effective governance can be achieved.*

At the core of the budget are people. A budget pertains to the utilization of financial resources to orchestrate human activities, so as to realize the collective welfare of the people. This implies that the metric for evaluating the efficacy of a budget is the people's sense of accessibility and sustainable development.

The key to rendering a budget effective lies in fully stimulating the enthusiasm and creativity of budget participants and identifying a judicious method for the allocation and utilization of public funds. All budgetary institutions should be designed from basic human nature to foster individual and communal development.

[Zhongyong] Therefore, governance is dependent on having the right people. You attract the right people by your own character. You cultivate your character through the Way and you manifest the Way by means of benevolence.

[Commentary] This passage references the preceding text - "when people are right, the government flourishes." The phrase "governance is dependent on people" encapsulates a comprehensive meaning. Here, the "right people" refer to sagacious officials, while "you" denotes the king. The Way is interpreted as the prevalent path. Benevolence, symbolizing the life-giving heart of Heaven and Earth, facilitates human survival. This implies that the king's governance is contingent upon winning the hearts of the people. The principle of engaging the people lies in self-cultivation. If one can cultivate oneself, then the roles of the king and the ministers will be fulfilled, and governance will not falter.*

The budget aims to promote holistic human development. Based on this goal, the government sets up various strategies, plans, tasks, and measures that require human participation. People are the key factor in the budget, and budget changes show changes in the budget participants.

No matter how grandiose or elaborate the budget model is, it won't work if the budget participants don't change their mindset and behavior to implement the development goals and actions. It merely represents a case of repackaging old concepts in new forms. Only by examining how the budget changes affect people's thinking and behavior can the budget move in the right direction.

[Zhongyong] Benevolence refers to humanity, and its principal manifestation is observed in the affection for kin. Righteousness refers to appropriateness, and its principal manifestation is exhibited in the reverence for the virtuous. The varying degrees of familial affection and respect for the virtuous are articulated through propriety.

[Commentary] The term "humanity" pertains to humaneness. Possessing humaneness naturally entails empathy and affection for others, which can be perceived with profound appreciation. The term "appropriateness" denotes "distinguishing matters in accordance with reason". "Propriety" relates to the conduct signified by these two concepts: affection and respect.*

The budget serves as a catalyst for social advancement, which in turn enhances the quality of life for individuals. It also fosters economic growth, thereby bolstering governmental and societal capabilities.

First, within the confines of fiscal resources, efforts should be made to improve people's wellbeing, such as the employment-first initiatives, quality education, social security, public health, cultural undertakings, and the strengthening of natural disaster prevention and relief measures.

Next, the transfer payment system can be fully tapped to enhance the livelihood support for poorer and less developed areas.

Further, budget spending should prioritize breaking technological bottlenecks and dependencies to boost economic independence and progress. To achieve this, the solutions encompass three facets.

1. Implementation of Innovation-supporting Policies: including taxation, asset management, government procurement, and finance.
2. Pooling of Funds: establishing an industrial and supply chain that is independent, controllable, safe, and stable.
3. Implementation of Government's Investment Incentives: establishing an ecosystem that adequately represents the value of innovative elements like knowledge and technology. which will further stimulate safe, high-quality, and sustainable economic development.

Just as trees have trunks and branches, everything in life has its hierarchy of significance. Hence, by strategically addressing the weakest areas and taking a long-term view, we can ensure the optimal use of finite budgetary resources for the greatest possible advantage.

[Zhongyong] In the absence of a high-ranking position and the backing of influential individuals, exerting influence over governmental operations becomes an unattainable aspiration.

[Commentary] Zheng Xuan (127-200) noted: "This sentence overlaps with the succeeding text."*

[Zhongyong] Therefore, the Noble Man cannot but cultivate his character. The desire to cultivate his character necessitates the service to his parents. The act of serving parents requires an understanding of others. This understanding of others is unattainable without comprehending the concept of Heaven."

[Commentary] Skillful governance is contingent upon having the right people, who are drawn by the character of the leader. Thus, the cultivation of one's character is imperative. This cultivation is achieved through the Way, and the Way is manifested via benevolence. Consequently, when contemplating the cultivation of character, one cannot neglect familial affection. To fulfill the obligation of kinship, one must first learn to revere the good, implying the necessity to understand others. The varying degrees of familial affection and venerating the good are all principles of Heaven. Therefore, understanding Heaven is essential.*

The budget should serve the public by following economic principles, supporting societal progress, adapting to environmental changes, and embracing scientific advances. It must manage risks, both internal and external, reflect the people's true needs and long-term interests, and promote openness, tolerance, and resilience to build consensus, encourage shared prosperity, resolve critical constraints, and ensure lasting stability. It should focus on the people's concerns and broader issues.

[Zhongyong] There exist five universal human relationships in the world, enacted through three virtues. These relationships encompass those between king and minister, father and son, husband and wife, elder and younger siblings, and among friends. The three virtues encompass wisdom, benevolence and courage, which are practiced in unison.

[Commentary] These five universal relationships are enduring principles upheld by humanity throughout history, referred to as the five ethics in *The Book of History*. Mencius elucidates these as "a caring father and a filial son, a benevolent king and a loyal minister, a harmonious husband and wife each fulfilling their respective duties, respect of younger siblings to the elder, and trust among friends." Wisdom pertains to understanding these relationships; benevolence involves experiencing these relationships; courage is about promoting these relationships. Collectively, they are recognized as the universal virtues, acknowledged by people throughout history. The crux of these virtues lies in sincerity. Despite the universal appreciation for the five universal relationships, their execution is impossible without the three virtues. Similarly, while people universally pursue the three universal virtues, if there is even a hint of insincerity, people's desires will infiltrate, and virtue will no longer be true virtue. The Masters Cheng said, "What is called sincerity is simply being truthful in these three aspects. Beyond these three, there is no other sincerity."*

The essence of a budget is its political aspect and how it allocates interests. Ideally, a budget should aim for harmony, not uniformity, considering the complex network of stakeholders, driven by values like empathy, justice, clarity, structure, and trust. There are three essential steps in the budgeting process.

The first step is to assess the budget's needs based on these relationships, which includes setting standards, defining the scope, and calculating the immediate and future financial needs.

The second step is to consider the funding sources, like taxes or fees, and how these funds are distributed. A preliminary budget should be drafted with clear strategies and goals, mindful of past obligations, present requirements, and future projections. It should aim for equity, unobscured by the veil of ignorance, promoting good over harm, and blending aspiration with practicality.

The final step involves making decisions and implementing them. Budgeting often entails negotiations and compromises, while execution can present obstacles that call for creative solutions and adaptability.

The budgeting process is cyclical, involving evaluation, planning, and action, shaping the budgetary framework and capabilities with a focus on the community's welfare. Continuous improvement and striving for excellence are essential for the budget's evolution.

[Zhongyong] Some know the three virtues inherently from birth; others know through learning, while some must grapple to know. Regardless, the essence of knowing remains consistent. Some practice them with ease; others practice them to enjoy their rewards, while some are compelled to practice them. However, once the practice is mastered, it is the same.

[Commentary] People know and practice the three virtues to attain the Way. From a classification perspective, those who know them are deemed wise, those who practice them are considered benevolent, and those who emulate successful examples are viewed as courageous. In terms of its level, the one who is naturally inclined to know and practice them comfortably is wise; the one who recognizes the advantage of learning and practicing them is benevolent; and the one who perceives its benefits amidst adversity and then endeavors to follow them is courageous. Despite the inherent goodness of all human nature, the degree of endowment can vary. Some might have been introduced to the Way earlier than others, and some may find it simpler to practice, but if one can persist in it despite difficulties and deficiencies, the ultimate outcome is identical. Lü Buwei (291–235 BCE) stated, "Commencing from diverse paths and converging to the same state embodies the principle of the mean. The Way remains elusive and seldom pursued because some harbor the hope of innate understanding, yet deem it beyond reach, while others, lacking the expectation of mastery through diligence, exert scant effort before yielding."*

The primary objective of the budget is to identify effective methods to allocate and use funds. Much of the budget is pre-determined by past decisions, making it best to follow existing guidelines. Some budgets become widely accepted programs, while others face challenges due to immediate needs and uncertain outcomes, which may only be clear after use or influenced by others' finances.

Budgeting is about planning for the future, and uncertainty makes balancing funds more challenging, requiring adjustments. Budgets evolve and require consensus; without it, conflicts arise. Indeed, the nature of a budget can be ambiguous, and its ultimate success often hinges on the ability to adapt and find a delicate balance between various factors and interests despite evolving circumstances.

[Zhongyong] The Master said: "With a fondness for learning, one nears wisdom; with a passion for vigorous practice, one nears benevolence. With comprehension of shame, one nears courage."

[Commentary] "The Master said" is redundant here. The text elaborated on how individuals did not possess virtue should continue to pursue it. In the preceding text, the three "knows" constitute wisdom, while the three "practices" constitute benevolence. Here, the three "nears" pertain to courage, completing the triad of virtues. Lü Buwei stated, "Fools are presumptuous and do not seek knowledge; selfish individuals are blinded by desire, and cowards willingly submit themselves to others without expressing their thoughts. Therefore, a love for learning is not wisdom in itself but is sufficient for individuals to shed their foolishness; a love for energetic practice is not benevolence in itself but is sufficient for individuals to forget their selfishness; understanding is not courage in itself but is sufficient for individuals to overcome their cowardice."*

The primary task of budgeting is to identify and understand its needs, which requires a deep knowledge of the program and precise evaluation, including comparison and future planning. Initially, applicants might find it challenging to apply the budget effectively or suggest viable ideas. Yet, they will truly know the budgetary preparation and make improvements after constant negotiations and updatings in the process of budgeting and decision-making based on standard procedure and requirements.

The secondary task relates to its execution. An effective system should be put in place to incentivize the budget managers and encourage collaboration among stakeholders, thus improving the budget's effectiveness and value for money.

The third task includes active oversight and consistent assessment, ensuring that any problems during execution are quickly detected and solved. The insights from these evaluations should be thoroughly applied to refine the existing budget or to better inform subsequent ones.

These three tasks are mutually reinforcing throughout the budget implementation cycle. Enhancing the budgetary preparation can improve execution, which in turn enriches comprehension of the budget. A systematic evaluation of the budget can inform and improve its implementation.

[Zhongyong] Upon comprehending these three elements, one gains insight into cultivating one's character; with the knowledge of cultivating one's character, one learns to manage other individuals; mastering the art of managing other individuals equips one with the skills to govern a state or clan.

[Commentary] These three elements correspond to the three aforementioned approaches. A state or nation comprises myriads of such individuals. This statement serves to conclude the preceding discussion on character cultivation and to introduce the forthcoming topic of the nine fundamental principles.*

The core aspects of budget capacity - understanding, execution, and enhancement - are interlinked. Boosting this capacity requires participants to improve these skills in the budget process. Beyond just budgeting, this calls for comprehensive reforms in government's recruitment and incentive mechanisms.

[Zhongyong] There exist nine fundamental principles in the governance of a state. These include self-cultivation of character, reverence for virtue, love for kin, respect for high-ranking ministers, motivating lower-ranking officers, paternal care for the common people, the welcoming of artisans, the gentle handling of distant guests, and the winning of loyalty of feudal lords.

[Commentary] These principles serve as the cardinal guides. Lü Buwei stated, "The foundation of a country lies within each individual, hence self-cultivation of character is the foundation. However, to refine one's character, it is necessary to venerate and learn from teachers and friends, thus placing the reverence for virtue second. The family is the priority for self-improvement through the Way, hence the love for kinship is ranked third. The court follows the family, leading to the respect for high-ranking ministers and the motivating of lower-ranking officers. The country follows the court, leading to the paternalistic treatment of the common people and the welcoming of artisans. The world follows the country, leading to the gentle handling of distant guests and the winning of the loyalty of feudal lords. This is the order of the nine principles of conduct." The distinction between treating ministers and treating the common people lies in treating ministers as extensions of oneself and treating the common people as one's children.*

The budget should energize all stakeholders. The people are the starting point and culmination of the budget process. Only through their active involvement can the budget reflect the nation's collective will.

The budget department, bearing the primary responsibility for budgeting, guarantees its ongoing improvement and execution. The finance department, as the budget's backbone, maintains its scale and structure through good coordination. Government leaders, central to the budget, provide clear guidance and focus through their sagacious command, while the legislative branch, acting as the budget's regulator, seeks excellence by harnessing collective wisdom.

The budget must address all interests, ensure basic services, and balance public and market forces. Additionally, a responsible nation must fulfill its global duties and consider the budget's worldwide effects.

[Zhongyong] By cultivating one's character, one establishes the Way. Revering virtue ensures freedom from delusion. Loving one's family prevents resentment among fathers, elder and younger brothers. Respecting high-ranking ministers prevents the occurrence of foolish errors. Including lower-ranking officers encourages them to regard propriety with seriousness. Treating the common people as one's children motivates them to work diligently. Welcoming artisans fosters a thriving commerce. Being gentle to distant guests attracts people from all directions. Favoring the nobility instills a healthy fear among the people.

[Commentary] These are the effects of the nine principles of conduct. Establishing one's own Way implies mastering the Way and serving as a model for the common people, which is also the method for a king to govern the country. Being free from delusion leaves no room for doubt about the truth. Avoiding foolish mistakes prevents confusion in any affair. Respecting high-ranking ministers leads to mutual trust, leaving no opportunity for treacherous ministers to cause division, and prevents foolish mistakes when dealing with state affairs. Welcoming artisans ensures that work can be accomplished easily, and artisans and merchants are willing to cooperate with each other, resulting in a thriving commerce. Being gentle to distant guests makes people around the world willing to visit, and over time, people will flock from all directions. Winning the loyalty of feudal lords leads more people to recognize your virtues and submit to your prestige, ultimately causing the whole world to hold you in awe.*

In the budget process, each participant has a role to play. The budget needs to be shared in a transparent, clear, detailed, and easily accessible manner, and public input is sought for key decisions. Budget departments shall get more control to improve budget performance management and evaluation systems. The finance department ought to strengthen oversight to mitigate financial risks, optimize the expenditure structure, and augment operational efficiency. Government leaders need to push for functional reforms, focus on major initiatives, and implement the new development strategies. The legislature should enhance oversight, allow more time for review, and improves the deliberation process.

[Zhongyong] Engaging in fasting while donned in ceremonial attire and adhering to the norms of propriety, these are the ways to cultivate one's character. Abandoning slander, liberating oneself from lust, disregarding wealth, and valuing virtue, these are the ways to revere virtue. Respecting their rank, compensating them adequately, and accommodating their preferences, these are the ways to love one's kin. Assigning them sufficient officers and delegating their responsibilities, these are the ways to respect high-ranking ministers. Rewarding trustworthiness and loyalty, these are the ways to motivate lower-ranking officers. Employing the people in accordance with their farming schedules and imposing light taxes, these are the ways to care for the people. Regularly examining their work and acknowledging merit where due, these are the ways to welcome artisans. Dispatching envoys to greet distant visitors and rewarding kindness and compassion to the handicapped, these are the ways

to gently treat visitors from afar. Restoring their disrupted lineages, reviving fallen states, managing chaos with caution, and safeguarding them from danger; bestowing them with generous gifts and expecting minimal return, these are the ways to win the loyalty of feudal lords.

> [Commentary] These are the specific actions that should be undertaken under the nine principles of conduct. Providing high-ranking ministers with enough officers to delegate their responsibilities implies assigning them sufficient subordinates to execute orders and missions, and this is likely because high-ranking ministers are not required to handle trivial matters. Rewarding trustworthiness and loyalty well entails treating lower-ranking officers with sincerity and offering them rewards, and this is likely because one has experienced firsthand and comprehended the type of ministers upon whom the lower-ranking officers rely. Examining the work of artisans akin to the officers in charge of food during the Zhou Dynasty, and it is what was referred to as "testing their crossbows and the result is used as a basis for increasing or decreasing the amount of food given to them." Dispatching envoys to bid farewell to distant visitors and preparing ample food and money to welcome incoming visitors aligns with the imperial regulation of "sending scholar-officials with tribute to the king every year, sending ministers with a tribute to the king every three years, and the nobles coming to have an audience with the king every five years". Bestowing generous gifts and expecting minimal return indicates that the king presents the nobility with an abundance of gifts and anticipates minimal tribute from them.*

Budgets are fundamentally grounded in principles. Deviating from these principles might offer immediate advantages, yet it almost always leads to detrimental long-term consequences. Maintaining fidelity to these principles is essential for ensuring the budget's robustness and integrity, which in turn helps to regulate the propensity for endless negotiations, as well as the scope and expenses associated with budgeting.

The budget is steered by the governance plan; although a bold plan may garner substantial resources, the foremost priority remains the stability of government financial reserves. Maintaining this stability requires careful consideration and strategic planning, as manifested in the following six areas:

First, major government policies, projects, and programs necessitate a highly sophisticated budget allocation strategy that incorporates temporal and spatial manipulation. Opportunities may be forfeited if no action is taken, yet exuberant actions often prove unsustainable.

Second, basic public services and social welfare constitute must expenditures, and once these expenditures are incurred, it becomes challenging to reverse them, thereby permanently constricting fiscal space.

Third, commitments made during times of financial prosperity often transform into liabilities during periods of financial hardship, necessitating the need for prudence and restraint.

Fourth, competitive pay levels in the public sector are crucial for attracting competent individuals to civil service. High-quality human resources can significantly elevate public service standards. To ensure effective government operations, a superior compensation package should be considered.

Fifth, reducing the tax burden can enhance the people's sense of fulfillment and the economy's competitiveness, and the impact of tax cuts must be balanced with high-quality economic development and superior government expenditure performance.

Sixth, as nations assume more international responsibilities, budget coverage will transcend national borders, necessitating budgets to be more adaptable and inclusive in the face of diverse political, economic, and cultural environments.

[Zhongyong] While there exist nine principles of conduct, a singular method underlies their execution.

[Commentary] This method is sincerity. In the absence of sincerity, these nine principles become vain. Sincerity constitutes the quintessence of these principles.*

The budget can only be precise, objective and sensible if budget participants articulate and act in a manner that is grounded in preciseness, objectivity and sensibility. Enhancing budget management, institutions, and mechanisms aims to foster a culture of preciseness, objectivity and sensibility among participants.

This entails a commitment to being realistic, maximizing effort, and working within means. It involves generating feasible revenues with a fair tax distribution, making prudent expenditures that align with social norms and performance metrics, and managing debts to ensure they don't compromise long-term stability.

[Zhongyong] In all endeavors, success is contingent upon prior planning, whereas the absence of planning invariably leads to failure. Preparedness prior to speaking precludes the possibility of being tongue-tied. Preparedness prior to commencing a task mitigates the risk of complications. Preparedness prior to action obviates the need for regret. Preparedness prior to teaching ensures a sufficient supply of material.

[Commentary] This discussion serves as a continuation from the preceding paragraph to underscore that sincerity is the prerequisite in all efforts, a point that is elaborated upon subsequently.*

A budget's soundness is pivotal to the success of an undertaking. It's crucial to ensure the budget's goals are clear, achievable, and essential. The budget plan should be systematic, focused, and well-organized. Ideal budget management is logical, uniform, transparent, and performance-driven. Budget targets should be accountable, exact, and challenging. Seen as an eco-system, the budget should encompass an undertaking or project's entire life cycle, integrating with various elements to optimize performance.

[Zhongyong] If one occupies a position of inferior rank without any influence over superiors, the ability to govern others is compromised. Even though there may be ways to influence superiors, if trust is lacking among peers, the ability to influence superiors is diminished. Similarly, even though there may be ways to earn the trust of peers, familial discord can undermine this trust. Even though there may be ways to foster harmony with kinship, reflecting on oneself and finding insincerity can lead to familial strife. Even though there may be ways to cultivate sincerity in character, without an inherent understanding of goodness, sincerity remains unattainable. When one holds a humble station, bereft of sway over those above, the governance of others falters. Though paths to sway superiors may exist, without trust among peers, such influence wanes. Likewise, though trust among peers may be sought, discord within the family can erode

this trust. Even if harmony with kin is pursued, self-reflection revealing insincerity can breed familial strife. And though one may strive to cultivate sincerity, without an innate grasp of goodness, true sincerity remains elusive.

[Commentary] This discussion refers to the context of a subordinate position, inferring the meaning of everyday planning. "Reflecting on oneself and finding insincerity" means to look back and examine oneself, realizing that what is maintained and expressed cannot be truly genuine. "Without an inherent understanding of goodness" means failing to comprehend the true nature of the human heart and the Mandate of Heaven, thus being unable to truly know what is the highest good. This discourse pertains to the context of a subordinate position, elucidating the essence of daily governance. "Reflecting on oneself and finding insincerity" signifies the act of introspection, wherein one discerns that what is upheld and conveyed lacks true genuineness. "Without an inherent understanding of goodness" implies a failure to grasp the true nature of the human heart and the Mandate of Heaven, thereby rendering one incapable of comprehending the highest good.*

For the budget department, the top priority is to elucidate the program's goals and tasks, which requires a blend of realism and ambition, to effectively execute budgetary responsibilities. A performance-driven budget allocation and a personnel incentive system needs to be put in place, which aims to foster a diverse yet coordinated mechanism, thereby stimulating the enthusiasm and creativity of all involved. The department must implement measures such as budget integration, project bundling, and re-engineering of departmental functions to significantly enhance the efficiency of inter-departmental synergy. The budgeting goals and tasks must align with the government's development plan and annual plan to fully realize its role in serving the people.

[Zhongyong] Sincerity is the Way of Heaven; the pursuit of sincerity is the Way of Man. If one can achieve sincerity effortlessly and without concern for its attainment, and conform to the Way, one is deemed a sage.

[Commentary] This discourse extends the theme of cultivating sincerity in one's character. Sincerity signifies being genuine and devoid of deceit, mirroring the true state of natural principles. The practice of sincerity involves the pursuit of genuineness and the absence of deceit, which is a human endeavor. The virtue of a sage aligns with heavenly principles. True sincerity means conforming to the Way effortlessly and naturally, without concern for its attainment. If one has not reached the level of a sage, it is impossible to be entirely free of selfish desires, and thus one's virtue cannot be wholly genuine. Therefore, if one can attain without concern, they should seek out their goodness to understand it. If one cannot conform to the Way effortlessly, they should steadfastly adhere to it to achieve sincerity. This is the Way of Man. Attaining without concern equates to innate knowledge; conforming to the Way effortlessly is akin to natural conduct. Discovering goodness and holding fast to it signifies the benefits of learning and practicing it.*

The base budget, shaped by negotiations and compromises, represents a tacit agreement among stakeholders. Changes to it signify shifts in fiscal realities and governance philosophies. While some budget increases are rational and uncontested, becoming integral to the base budget, others, lacking consensus, mirror the victors' views in fiscal negotiations, unsupported by other factions. Their future acceptance hinges on practical outcomes and collective understanding.

Comprehending the base budget is key to grasping fiscal strategies; however, overreliance on it can hinder necessary responses to evolving realities. Historically, zero-based budgeting has facilitated resource redistribution and significant reforms. Post-reform, the base budget emerges anew as the guiding consensus in fiscal planning.

[Zhongyong] One must learn broadly, investigate meticulously, contemplate carefully, discern clearly, and practice earnestly.

[Commentary] This encapsulates the essence of sincerity. Throughout the process of learning, investigating, contemplating, and discerning, one uncovers both goodness and wisdom, thereby demonstrating that learning engenders wisdom. Earnest practice and steadfast adherence lead to the discovery of benevolence, signifying that learning yields benefits. The Masters Cheng said, "The absence of any of these five actions renders the learning process incomplete."*

The budgeting process demands the integration of knowledge and action. Without broad learning, it is impossible to fully grasp the budget situation. Without investigating meticulously, it is impossible to deeply understand the scope and standards of the budget. Without careful contemplation, it is impossible to pragmatically propose a budget plan. Without clear discernment, it is impossible to effectively allocate budget revenues and expenditures. Without earnest practice, it is impossible to strictly adhere to budget authorization and ensure serious budget execution, thereby achieving budget performance.

It is worth noting that the budget cycle is an interconnected system where each phase impacts the other; the efficacy of budgetary preparation influences its execution, which in turn shapes future budgeting and fiscal decisions. The appropriateness of budgetary benchmarks and scope also affects the overall budgeting process and its implementation.

[Zhongyong] When there is something one has yet to learn or master, one should not cease. When there is something one has yet to investigate or fully understand, one should not cease. When there is something one has yet to discern or insights remain obscured, one should not cease. Likewise, when there is something one has yet to practice or applications remain inconsistent, one should not cease. If someone else achieves it in one attempt, I will strive one hundred times. If someone else achieves it in ten attempts, I will strive one thousand times.

[Commentary] When the gentleman resolves to learn, he won't stop until he attains the goal, exerting efforts a hundredfold greater than others. True courage lies in acquiring knowledge despite difficulties and striving to practice what he has learned.*

Striving for excellence is essential in budgeting, which is key to fostering development. A deep grasp of the business landscape ensures effective resource allocation, plan execution, and outcome assessment, whether in asset management or in asset-business integration. This involves a deep understanding of the following facets.

First, budgetary challenges often arise from systemic flaws, highlighting the need to address not just immediate concerns but also to reform institutions for lasting stability. Take budget performance reform for example. While developing performance indicators and evaluation structures is important, the key lies in how to motivate the budget department. Establishing a reasonable mechanism can lead to broader reforms. The overarching objective of budget reform is to modernize governance structures and capacities. This requires coordinated efforts with human resource and asset management reforms oriented toward efficacy; otherwise, the reform endeavors are liable to falter.

In reality, effective budget management involves wisely granting autonomy to departments, with clear roles and incentives. Meaningful budgetary changes require ongoing effort and refinement. Unfortunately, there's a tendency for hasty involvement and abandonment when faced with obstacles, leading to restarts under new guises.

For instance, the medium-term budget around the year 2000 is an example of "much ado about nothing", making a grand entrance but yielding little in terms of results. It saw fragmented efforts, with the finance department working alone, planning department indifferent, and budgeting department directionless. Emphasizing procedural formalities overshadow the essence of the tasks at hand invariably results in flashy but fruitless projects.

In retrospect, the key steps towards effective reform lie in the basics that integrate planning and budgeting, aligning financial forecasts with development goals, and systematically creating project databases.

[Zhongyong] Should one follow the Way, even the unintelligent can attain enlightenment, and the weak can cultivate strength.

[Commentary] The pursuit of virtue leads to enlightenment, while steadfast adherence to virtue fosters strength. As articulated by Lü Buwei, the gentleman pursues learning to refine their temperament. Should one's moral character eclipse their inherent temperament, despite perceived intellectual deficiency, enlightenment is attainable, and strength can be acquired despite apparent weakness. Otherwise, one is unable to transcend folly and frailty even if he pursues learning. This might stem from human's intrinsic inclination towards goodness, which is the same nature human beings share. Yet, temperaments of individuals can be bright or dark, strong or weak. Their natural talents vary. Sincere individuals endeavor to transform these differences, so as to return to the same. Born to be untalented, one cannot transform his temperament unless he does his utmost. People today, however, are impetuous and irresponsible in their sporadic endeavors to rectify temperament deficiencies; once they have failed, they blame it on their nature and claim that learning cannot effect change. As a result, they abandon learning and change - an attitude incongruent with the concept of benevolence.*

By constantly improving budgeting systems, fiscal capabilities, resource allocation, and the standardization and effectiveness of budget execution, and controlling financial risks, the budget can effectively contribute to the modernization of governance systems and capacities.

[Commentary] The preceding text constitutes the twentieth chapter. This passage quotes Confucius' words, inheriting the work of the great Shun, King Wen of Zhou, King Wu of Zhou, and the Duke of Zhou, which illustrates their consistent transmission and practical application. This includes discussions on the extensiveness and subtlety, the large and the small, to complete the meaning of Chapter 12. Notably, this chapter begins a detailed discussion on sincerity, with sincerity serving as its central theme. According to *Kongzi Jiayu* (The School Sayings of Confucius), this chapter is also recorded there, wherein its contents are particularly detailed. Below the expression "when the practice is mastered, it is the same" is the remark of Duke Ai of Lu: "The master's words are admirable and perfect but I am too ignorant to perfect the practice." This is followed by "The Master said" again to introduce the response. The interrogative speech is not present here, but the words 'The Master said' remain. This is probably a derivative when Zisi failed to delete it in his attempt to remove the redundant text, so it should now be considered interpolated text. Given that there is no more content after the phrase "One must learn broadly" in *The School Sayings of Confucius*, the other written parts may be missing or perhaps Zisi complemented them in the passage.*

The interplay between a budget system and its capacity is crucial for sound fiscal governance. An efficient budget system not only nurtures the abilities of its stakeholders but also allows them to influence the system itself. This synergy is essential for improving budgetary outcomes.

Within governmental frameworks, budget systems are subject to various interpretations and applications, reflecting a spectrum of viewpoints. A skilled stakeholder can optimize an average budget system for success, whereas those with hidden agendas might manipulate even the most well-designed systems for personal gain.

Budget systems are underpinned by complex networks of interests and interpersonal dynamics. Reforms target these undercurrents to alleviate conflicts and establish checks and balances that promote healthy competition. The diversity in budget systems and capacities creates unique operational environments, calling for tailored approaches over one-size-fits-all solutions.

Setting explicit performance targets and defining stakeholder roles are equally important; lacking clear goals or defined roles can lead to unachieved objectives and operational challenges. The core purpose of a budget system is to act as a strategic framework that generates public value, enables personal growth, and encourages higher aspirations.

This role is multifaceted, involving:

1. Setting budgetary regulations to control actions, timing, and compliance with internal controls;
2. Defining performance goals and assessment metrics, underscoring accountability and conscientious budget execution;
3. Authorizing managers to allocate funds thoughtfully, in line with real needs, and encouraging both standardization and innovation;
4. Coordinating budget distribution with specific tasks to harmonize financial, human, and material resources;
5. Creating incentives to enhance resource efficiency and effectiveness;
6. Constructing a revenue system that aligns public welfare with economic expansion;
7. Implementing strict cost controls to reduce waste and maintain fiscal discipline;
8. Using budgetary policies to support growth in disadvantaged regions and strengthen social unity;

9. Distributing funds to meet international commitments and foster global collaboration.

At the core of these dimensions is a dedication to budgetary integrity, adherence to core principles, and meticulous execution, supported by continuous learning, critical reflection, and prudent decision-making.

This cyclical process requires steadfastness and gradual progress, especially when performing fundamental tasks that provide long-term advantages, such as honing performance goals and carefully evaluating expenses. These efforts are the bedrock of proficient budgetary governance.

Chapter 21
The Return to Budgeting

[Zhongyong] Enlightenment born of sincerity can be ascribed to nature. Sincerity born of enlightenment can be ascribed to education. Sincerity inherently leads to enlightenment, and enlightenment fosters sincerity.

> [Commentary] The virtue of a sage is genuine and enlightens everything, reflecting the true nature of the Way. This virtue is inherent in their nature and aligns with the Way of Heaven. Understanding goodness first, and then enriching it, is the pursuit of the virtuous, achieved through education and representing the Way of Man. Sincerity leads to complete enlightenment, and enlightenment leads to sincerity. *

The budget fundamentally serves the people, aiming to fulfill their collective desire for a better life. While the scope of the budget is comprehensive and its goals varied, its ultimate measure of success lies in its ability to address the people's fundamental needs. The more effectively the budget mirrors and actualizes the people's core and widespread aspirations throughout its formulation, the higher its quality. Therefore, the design of the budget system and the development of budgetary competencies must adhere to this guiding principle, ensuring that every fiscal decision advances the public's well-being.

> [Commentary] The preceding text constitutes the twenty-first chapter. Continuing from Confucius's perspective in the aforementioned chapter on the Way of Heaven and the Way of Man, Zisi further elucidated this notion across the subsequent twelve chapters. *

The budget must reflect its foundational ethos, serving as the fuel for government operations. A strong budgetary structure is built on a cohesive governance framework, where improvements in budgetary function are matched by advancements in governance.

Note: The paragraphs marked with an asterisk (*) are sourced from Zhu Xi's *Sishu Zhangju Jizhu* (Collected Commentaries on the Four Books), specifically *Zhongyong Zhangju* (Commentaries on the Zhongyong), Chapter 21, pages 32–33.

Y. Gou, *The Mean in Budgeting*, https://doi.org/10.1007/978-981-96-9592-8_21

Yet, real-world scenarios often reveal discrepancies and inefficiencies, marked by difficulties in managing revenues and expenditures, lackluster execution of development agendas, and untapped managerial potential. These issues obstruct the attainment of budgetary goals and hinder the evolution of governance mechanisms.

Evolving trends, governance challenges, and shifts in economy and society as well as in practitioners' minds, can catalyze reforms that realign the budget.

For instance, in the late 1990s, robust fiscal growth prompted reforms like soft budget constraints and departmental budget restructuring. These measures successfully consolidated and balanced in-budgets and off-budgets, centralized management, and improved budgeting precision.

Following the 2008 financial crisis, medium-term budget frameworks were introduced, requiring budget departments to prepare a three-year budget at one time and use the medium-term framework to constrain the annual budget.

In practice, however, it yielded modest results, due to discrepancies between planning and budgeting, as well as lack of predictive accuracy and cross-departmental collaboration.

Today, the quest for budgetary performance management faces challenges like lukewarm departmental engagement, superficial goals, and cursory self-evaluations, which undermine effective supervision and administration.

The heart of the issue is the lack of departmental accountability, independence, and drive. Addressing this requires a dedicated effort to strengthen governance structures and capabilities. Budget departments should have clearly-defined rights and accountability systems, based on measurable or justifiable performance indicators.

Additionally, providing departments with the autonomy to manage projects and resources, is crucial for boosting transparency and effectiveness. Ultimately, the success of budgetary performance management depends on balancing power with responsibility, granting departments the autonomy needed for innovation and creativity in public service. When coupled with performance-linked incentives, this autonomy can lead to significant shifts in governance outcomes.

All in all, achieving budgetary success demands a collective dedication to excellence and accountability from all budget departments.

Chapter 22
The Logic of Budgeting

[Zhongyong] Only individuals with perfect sincerity can fulfill their own nature. Being able to fulfill their own nature, they can fulfill the nature of others. Being able to fulfill the nature of others, they can fulfill the nature of all things. Being able to fulfill the nature of all things, they can assist Heaven and Earth in their transformation and sustenance. Being able to assist in Heaven and Earth's transformation and sustenance, they form a trinity with Heaven and Earth.

[Commentary] The phrase "perfect sincerity" refers to the true virtue of a sage, which surpasses all others. "Fulfilling their own nature" means that virtue is entirely genuine, free from selfish desires, and that what is endowed by Heaven is fully understood and followed, with nothing left undeveloped, whether large or small, fine or coarse. The nature of humans and things is also my nature, differing only due to the physical and temperamental endowments. "Fulfilling" means achieving complete knowledge and perfectly appropriate actions. "Assisting in Heaven and Earth's transformation and sustenance" refers to standing alongside Heaven and Earth as one of the three. This represents the sage's journey from sincerity to enlightenment. *

Optimizing budgetary resources hinges on recognizing their latent potential, which is deeply connected to human capabilities. In turn, the realization of human potential depends on how these resources are employed. To foster comprehensive growth in human abilities and optimize the use of physical resources, we need institutional structures that allow for the expression of human nature in budgeting activities. Through such frameworks, we can unlock the full promise of these resources. Advancing budgetary processes calls for a re-engagement with our innate human qualities in optimizing budgetary resources.

[Commentary] The preceding text constitutes the twenty-second chapter. This chapter discusses the Way of Heaven. *

Note: The paragraphs marked with an asterisk (*) are sourced from Zhu Xi's *Sishu Zhangju Jizhu* (Collected Commentaries on the Four Books), specifically *Zhongyong Zhangju* (Commentaries on the Zhongyong), Chapter 22, page 33.

Y. Gou, *The Mean in Budgeting*, https://doi.org/10.1007/978-981-96-9592-8_22

Establishing budget targets is critical. The essence of departmental budgeting is not found in its operational mechanics but in its performance, without which departmental budgeting is essentially aimless. Identifying necessary actions and avoiding counterproductive ones is crucial when establishing performance targets. These targets must align with the departmental duties and fiscal resources, and they should be challenging yet achievable.

Moreover, creating a space where talents and resources are maximized is crucial for realizing performance targets. By optimizing organizational structures and incentives, we can tap into the collective ambition and skills of budgetary department staff, empowering them to responsibly exercise their authority and adhere to rules.

Chapter 23
The Improvement of Budgeting

[Zhongyong] The individuals with near perfect sincerity can attain goodness in specific areas. With their goodness in specific areas, they can possess sincerity. With sincerity, they have form. Having form, their sincerity becomes manifest. Being manifest, the sincerity becomes brilliant. Being brilliant, it can move. Moving, it effects changes. By changing, it transforms. Only the most fulfilled sincerity can transform people and things.

[Commentary] The term "individuals of near perfect sincerity" refers to all those who are not as virtuous as the great sages. While human nature is fundamentally the same, differences in temperament exist. Only sages can fully realize their nature. Those who do not possess perfect sincerity must cultivate the shoots of goodness and strive to attain it. When goodness is attained in all aspects, virtue becomes genuine, and the efforts to have form, to become manifest, to move, and to change do not cease. When accumulated to the point of influencing others, their profound sincerity becomes indistinguishable from that of the sages. *

Improvement in the budget process can be approached systematically or initiated from a specific angle, building incrementally. Excellent budgetary preparation allows for coordination between preparation and execution, leading to effective budget implementation. This progression naturally extends to auditing and evaluation, which are indispensable for assessing the quality of the budget process.

Without superior planning and execution, auditing and evaluation become futile—akin to a skilled cook lacking ingredients. The budget cannot operate in isolation; it does not dictate itself. It is shaped and reshaped by policy shifts, institutional reforms, and management changes, necessitating adaptive adjustments to fulfill policy goals, optimize institutions, and elevate management practices.

Similarly, alterations in budget allocation models and financial assurances introduce fresh prospects and hurdles across various sectors. Without thorough and

---

Note: The paragraphs marked with an asterisk (*) are sourced from Zhu Xi's *Sishu Zhangju Jizhu* (Collected Commentaries on the Four Books), specifically *Zhongyong Zhangju* (Commentaries on the Zhongyong), Chapter 23, page 33.

Y. Gou, *The Mean in Budgeting*, https://doi.org/10.1007/978-981-96-9592-8_23

thoughtful evaluation, reforms may backfire. Even a minor managerial enhancement, if precisely targeted, can lead to significant global improvements, whereas a grand but ill-conceived initiative is bound to fail.

[Commentary] The preceding text constitutes the twenty-third chapter. This chapter discusses the Way of Man. *

Strengthening budgetary capacity is a complex task that requires dedicated effort and commitment. Given the nuanced interplay of cultural and traditional factors in budgetary processes, meaningful progress is achieved through a unified approach that combines strategic initiatives and practical improvements. The success of such transformation relies on strong political support, steadfast dedication, and strict management protocols.

Since 2012, the government has been enforcing the "Eight-point Decision on Governmental Conduct" to revamp work practices and enhance public relations. This policy has led to significant savings in government operational costs and a reduction in budgets concerning three public expenses: public spending on overseas trips, official receptions, and buying and using government cars.

Despite initial doubts, consistent application and enforcement have led to broad acceptance and adherence among civil servants, reflecting a shift in governmental conduct driven by effective regulation and public involvement.

The full adoption of budget performance management in 2018 marks a deliberate move to update governance structures and improve fiscal control, planning, and management. Echoing the rigorous nature of the Eight-point Decision, effective budget performance management also demands stringent standards to cultivate the right mindset among officials and encourage ongoing innovation.

Aligning fiscal strategies and actions with performance goals is crucial, yet it presents the challenge of balancing these goals with necessary control measures. Addressing this requires a comprehensive strategy that marries performance incentives with strong oversight.

Chapter 24
The Practice of Budgeting

[Zhongyong] The Way of perfect sincerity entails foreknowledge. When a nation is destined to rise, there are always good omens. When a nation is destined to fall, there are always evil omens. These signs can be seen in the milfoil stalks, tortoise shells or from the movement of people's four limbs. When good or evil fortune is imminent, those with perfect sincerity will invariably know. With perfect sincerity, one is akin to a deity.

[Commentary] Good omens are signs of prosperity; evil omens are the seeds of disaster. The milfoil stalks are used for divination; the tortoise shell is used to predict good fortune. The four limbs refer to human movements and postures, such as the height at which one holds jade, bowing, and other gestures. All these are manifestations of principles that appear before the events themselves. However, only those who have reached the utmost sincerity, without a trace of selfish or false thoughts in their minds, can discern the signs and beginnings of fortune and disaster. *

A robust budget is rooted in solid fiscal philosophies and principles. Small departures from these guiding tenets can lead to substantial variances. Political, economic, and global forces significantly shape budgetary decisions, demanding thoughtful and strategic responses. It's crucial to distinguish between appropriate adjustments and excessive reactions. Abandoning core principles for short-term gains is counterproductive, much like quenching thirst with poison. Instead, adhering to these principles while strategically adapting to changes offers a more sustainable approach, ensuring long-term success and a position ahead of the curve.

[Commentary] The preceding text constitutes the twenty-fourth chapter. This chapter discusses the Way of Heaven. *

A budget must be visionary yet grounded in reality. The true test of its efficacy lies in practice. The feasibility of achieving a well-conceived plan hinges on the

---

Note: The paragraphs marked with an asterisk (*) are sourced from Zhu Xi's *Sishu Zhangju Jizhu* (Collected Commentaries on the Four Books), specifically *Zhongyong Zhangju* (Commentaries on the Zhongyong), Chapter 24, page 34.

Y. Gou, *The Mean in Budgeting*, https://doi.org/10.1007/978-981-96-9592-8_24

budget's appeal, foresight, and practicality, as well as its ability to navigate inevitable uncertainties.

A well-crafted budget can enhance prosperity and transform crises into stability; conversely, a poorly constructed budget can exacerbate challenges. Ultimately, the key is not the current state of affairs but the development and ongoing refinement of the budget system and its capacity to dynamically seize opportunities and address issues.

In prosperous times, the temptation to increase spending is high, and without prudent foresight, this can lead to unsustainable practices. In tougher economic conditions, consensus on fiscal restraint makes budgetary controls more palatable, emphasizing the need to resist overcorrection and maintain stability while awaiting improvement.

Accurate and relevant information is the cornerstone of an effective budget. Different stakeholders require tailored budget data: decision-makers need performance targets and metrics linked to budgetary needs, budget departments require comprehensive project details and implementation strategies, and the public seeks thorough insights into areas of interest. Success depends on customizing information to meet the diverse needs of decision-making, execution, and oversight.

By steadfastly upholding fundamental budgetary principles across various fiscal landscapes, we can refine budgetary reasoning, maintain fiscal discipline, and simplify complex budgetary management. This approach prevents repeated concessions to external pressures, ensuring that budgetary practices do not stray from their intended course.

Chapter 25
Budget Performance

[Zhongyong] Sincerity is self-fulfillment, while the Way is self-direction.

[Commentary] This section explains that sincerity is the basis for things to achieve their own nature, while the Way is the path individuals must traverse of their own accord. Sincerity represents the heart, the essence, while the Way represents the principles, which are applied. *

What constitutes the budget's essence, and what lies within its domain? How is a budget formed and how does it evolve? The creation and progression of budgets, through ongoing cycles of growth and adjustment, represent a persistent quest to address these fundamental issues. The varied questions foster diverse budgetary structures. Because there are no identical questions, there are no identical budgets. Superficial similarities in budget processes can lead to significantly varied fiscal results.

[Zhongyong] Sincerity is the beginning and end of things; without sincerity, there is nothing. Therefore, the Noble Man values sincerity above all.

[Commentary] All things in the world are created by true principles, so one must obtain these principles before the things themselves can exist. If these principles are lost, the things will also cease to exist. Therefore, if a person's heart has even a slight falsehood, their actions, though seemingly significant, are essentially meaningless. Thus, a gentleman must regard sincerity as the most precious thing. As long as the heart is free from falsehood, one's actions will surely succeed, and the Way in one's heart will be fully realized. *

The budget is people-oriented and should actively respond to the people's aspiration for a better life. Major arrangements and adjustments of government budget revenue and expenditure should heed public sentiment, ensuring its alignment with the public interests. Taxation and levies should be managed to afford individuals greater economic agency, thereby stimulating economic growth. Fiscal policies

Note: The paragraphs marked with an asterisk (*) are sourced from Zhu Xi's *Sishu Zhangju Jizhu* (Collected Commentaries on the Four Books), specifically *Zhongyong Zhangju* (Commentaries on the Zhongyong), Chapter 25, page 34.

Y. Gou, *The Mean in Budgeting*, https://doi.org/10.1007/978-981-96-9592-8_25

should be anchored in the overarching objective of advancing societal progress, while expenditure allocations should embody principles of equity and impartiality. Essential public services should be directed towards addressing practical challenges such as rectifying regional, urban-rural, and income disparities. Furthermore, major policies and projects should focus on the people's sense of access, happiness and security. Budget performance information should be open and transparent, understandable and accountable.

[Zhongyong] Sincerity is not just self-fulfillment; it also means fulfilling all things. Fulfilling oneself is benevolence. Fulfilling things is wisdom. The virtue of our nature is the Way by which inner and outer are integrated. Thus, we can always use it to set things right.

[Commentary] Though sincerity begins with self-fulfillment, it naturally extends to encompass all things, thereby allowing "the Way" to be practiced universally. Benevolence signifies the essence of the self, while wisdom represents its application. Both virtues are innate within our nature, undifferentiated between internal and external realms. Once attained, they manifest according to circumstances, ensuring that all things are in their rightful place. *

The budget should focus on people. As people are different from each other, the budget should also pursue harmony while staying diverse, trying to ensure that all parties obtain what they need, and that the fairness and justice of the budget revenue and expenditure are achieved through stratification and classification.

No governmental entity exists in isolation from the global community; thus, the prosperity and advancement of individuals within a particular nation are intricately intertwined with those in other regions and countries. The sustainable development of all nations contributes to a collective prosperity beneficial to all global citizens.

Additionally, the budget must consider broader contextual factors, including technological advancements and eco-friendliness, which significantly impact human well-being. In the intricate international landscape, pivotal technologies often dictate a nation's trajectory, thereby influencing the people's happiness. Therefore, prioritizing strategic emerging technologies within the budgetary framework reflects a people-centered approach.

Throughout human history, a symbiotic relationship between humanity and nature has been emphasized, wherein mutual prosperity is achieved through harmonious coexistence. Consequently, the essence of the budget lies in aligning with the natural order, thereby fostering human flourishing.

By leveraging the budget's pivotal role in orchestrating economic, social, natural, and cultural resources for the betterment of individuals and society, it becomes instrumental in nurturing both human prosperity and the vitality of entities, enabling a state of contentment and fulfillment among the people.

[Commentary] The preceding text constitutes the twenty-fifth chapter. This chapter discusses the Way of Man. *

Budget performance is the self-fulfillment of the budgeters. The budget mechanism allocates funds, specifying their way of use, standards, and scope, which is the physical arrangement, but the key to transforming all this into the ultimate public service performance lies in people, and only the users of funds can turn stones into gold.

The definition of budge performance in terms of quantity and quality is only a presupposition to be falsified, and the users of funds may push the boundaries of performance a little further by being realistic, innovative and creative, and doing their best.

Budget performance is the self-fulfillment of budget participants. While the budget delineates funds allocation, utilization parameters, standards, and extent, the efficacy of these allocations in delivering public services is contingent upon human agency. Only through the adept utilization of allocated funds that tangible outcomes are achieved.

Budge performance in terms of quantity and quality serves only as initial benchmarks subject to revision, with users of funds capable of pushing performance boundaries through pragmatic, innovative, and creative approaches, thereby optimizing outcomes.

Chapter 26
Budget Governance

[Zhongyong] Therefore, perfect sincerity is ceaseless.

[Commentary] In the absence of falsehood, there exists an uninterrupted continuity.*

The budget operates akin to a continuous river, advancing day and night, never stopping. Current decisions and actions bear enduring implications, as any expedient measures are bound to misallocate resources and underperform.

The budget should adhere to the basic principle and respond to the needs of reality, and learn from past experiences, facilitating refinement over successive iterations. This iterative refinement aims to achieve a balanced scale, rational structure, moderate complexity, and standardized management practices within the budgetary framework.

[Zhongyong] Ceaseless, it is long-lasting. Long-lasting, it is evident.

[Commentary] Long-lasting endurance resides at the core, while evidence manifests outwardly.*

Profound changes in the budget require persistent efforts. The change of budget mindset, the adjustment of interest structure, and the development of managerial competencies can never be achieved overnight. It takes time to identify optimal conceptual frameworks, discover the right methodologies in repeated trial and error, and then, gradually perfect them in time.

[Zhongyong] Evident, it is far-reaching. Far-reaching, it is extensive and profound. Extensive and profound, it is high and bright.

[Commentary] These are the external manifestations as articulated by Zheng Xuan: "The virtue of perfect sincerity is visible to all." The longer it remains at the center, the more

Note: The paragraphs marked with an asterisk (*) are sourced from Zhu Xi's *Sishu Zhangju Jizhu* (Collected Commentaries on the Four Books), specifically *Zhongyong Zhangju* (Commentaries on the Zhongyong), Chapter 26, pages 34–36.

Y. Gou, *The Mean in Budgeting*, https://doi.org/10.1007/978-981-96-9592-8_26

far-reaching and infinite its external manifestations become. As it extends, its accumulation grows broad and profound; being extensive and profound, its external manifestation is elevated and radiant.*

The foundational components of the budget, encompassing budgetary preparation, revenue and expenditure categorization, decision-making processes, institutional structures, implementation protocols, as well as audit and evaluation frameworks, among others, demand a systemic, rational, and efficacious approach.

These arrangements, involving comprehensive engagement from governmental entities and stakeholders, necessitate systematic planning and continual refinement, eschewing ad hoc adjustments and inconsistencies.

Given its inherently political nature, the budget must be pragmatic, duly considering the interests of all stakeholders and the managerial capacity of the government. Moreover, it serves as a vehicle to realize political aspirations, providing a powerful pivot and a solid foundation for the modernization of governance structures and capacities.

[Zhongyong] Being extensive and profound, it can support all things. Being high and bright, it can cover all things. Since it is far-reaching and long-lasting, it can accomplish all things.

[Commentary] Being far-reaching and long-lasting is being extensive and profound, which refers to the Way by which inner and outer are merged. Being far-reaching leads to being high and profound, which is long-lasting. These words suggest that the sage is on par with Heaven and Earth.*

The budget should be extensive, profound, and realistic, grounded in China's unique context and fostering inclusive development. Additionally, it should exhibit height and brilliance, guided by forward-looking integrated planning to address fundamental needs and tackle pivotal challenges. Furthermore, the budget should be long-lasting and steady, controlling financial risks and achieving sustainable development. The basic features of the trinity of the budgetary realm are extensive and profound, high and bright, and far-reaching and long-lasting.

[Zhongyong] Extensiveness and profoundness correspond to the Earth. Highness and brightness correspond to Heaven. Far-reaching and long-lasting signify limitlessness.

[Commentary] This indicates that the sage embodies the same qualities as the Heaven and the Earth.*

The budget should be as extensive and profound as the earth, supporting everything; it should be as high and bright as the sky, encompassing everything; it should be as long-lasting as time, accomplishing everything.

[Zhongyong] In this way, it is evident without being seen, changes without moving, and accomplishes without action.

[Commentary] To be seen is also to be shown. It is evident without being seen, like the broad earth. It changes without moving, like the vast sky. It accomplishes without action, and such accomplishments are boundless.*

The budget is extensive and profound, high and bright, and far-reaching and long-lasting. The budget department takes charge and manages the finances, laying a solid foundation for achieving budgetary excellence and performance.

By adhering to prescribed rules, policies, institutions, mechanisms, processes, and standards, resources can be optimally allocated and efficiently utilized, ensuring orderly fiscal flow. The recurring intervention and guidance from the budget management department underscore the imperfection of the budgetary system, signaling the necessity for enhanced budgetary capacity.

The ideal state of the budget is to govern without effort, to do one's own job, and to make one's own accomplishments.

[Zhongyong] The Way of Heaven and Earth can be succinctly captured in the axiom: "Its manifestation in phenomena is singular, hence its generation of phenomena is unfathomable."

[Commentary] Consequently, the perpetual embodiment of perfect sincerity finds elucidation through the Way of Heaven and Earth, which can be epitomized by the concept of sincerity. Its sincerity is evidenced by its singleness, persisting incessantly, and its prolific generation of phenomena, wherein the rationale behind its eternal nature remains enigmatic to many.*

The budget should make sure its goals are constantly refined, exploiting resources in a precise and pure way. Various interest parties compete and cooperate in the budget with incompatible goals. Therefore, proactive efforts are necessary to identify, unite, and cultivate consensus, aligning partial interests with overarching goals, general interests with critical priorities, and short-term objectives with long-term visions. By refining budgetary goals and projects to enhance focus and specificity, the level of resource allocation within the budget can ascend to new heights of effectiveness and efficiency.

Budgeting requires the goals to be continuously refined, and resources be used precisely. Within the budgetary framework, various interests, representing divergent and incongruous goals, vie and collaborate. During the budgeting process, we should strive to identify common ground, and build consensus, overlaying local interests with global ones, general interests with paramount ones, and short-term interests with long-term ones. Only with more consolidated and clearer budget goals that we can elevate the allocation efficiency of budgetary resources, thereby paving the way for a more prosperous and promising future.

[Zhongyong] The Way of Heaven and Earth is extensive and profound, high and bright, far-reaching and long-lasting.

[Commentary] The Way of Heaven and Earth operates with sincerity and singularity, enabling all things on earth to function to their fullest, thereby bringing life to this world, as expounded in the following section.*

The Way of budgeting is extensive, profound, high, bright, far-reaching, and long-lasting. It constantly improves itself with great vitality.

[Zhongyong] Now, the sky may be just an accumulation of small patches of light, yet in its infiniteness, the sun, moon and stars are all encompassed in it, and all the things are covered by it. The earth may be an accumulation of handfuls

of dirt, yet in its extensiveness and profoundness, it bears up Mt. Hua and Mt. Yue without feeling weighty; it contains the seas and rivers without spilling a drop. It supports all things. The mountains may be just an accumulation of many small stones, yet in their height and size, plants and trees grow on them, the birds and beasts live on them, and rare gems are deposited within them. The waters may be just an accumulation of many spoons of water, yet in their boundlessness, tortoises, alligators, dragons, fish and turtles live there, and all sorts of commodities are produced there.

[Commentary] In this paragraph, "infiniteness" shares the same meaning as "ultimate form" denoted in chapter twelve, which represents the whole. These four things are mentioned to express the meaning of becoming broad and vigorous because of their singleness and ceaselessness, thereby supporting all things. However, the sky, earth, mountains, and rivers are not actually enlarged by accumulation, and the reader must not misinterpret the meanings because of the above figurative expressions.*

Budgets encompass a broad domain and follow cyclical patterns. Wherever there is government, a budget necessarily follows. Budgets are not static or immutable; they are in a state of constant flux and unpredictability.

Initiating processes is straightforward, yet few reaches fruition. A meticulously crafted budget may soon become antiquated, its content paling beneath its grand exterior; a seemingly innocuous expenditure may metamorphose into a substantial burden, and once initiated, there is no reversal.

We must exercise caution with every fiscal inflow and outflow. We need to ascertain its origin, evaluate its continued existence, determine its allocation, assess its financial sustainability amidst rapid growth, and consider its political necessity.

In the short term, there appears to be limited scope for maneuvering revenue and expenditure, particularly for main taxes and fundamental expenditure. In the long term, nothing is perpetual. Everything is subject to change and ought to change, and an appropriate budget serves as the pathway through the wilderness that leads to the future.

[Zhongyong] ***The Book of Songs*** **says: "The Mandate of Heaven is ever dignified and ceaseless." Such is why Heaven is Heaven. "Ah, how brilliant! The virtue of King Wen is pure." Such is why King Wen is King Wen, and his purity is also ceaseless."**

[Commentary] This is a passage in "The Mandate of Heaven" section within the chapter of "Odes of Zhou" in *The Book of Songs*. All the aforementioned poems are emblematic of sincerity and ceaselessness. The Masters Cheng asserted, "The Way of Heaven is ceaseless, and King Wen faithfully follows the Way of Heaven, so he is ceaseless." "Purity" is synonymous with singleness devoid of any contamination, and "ceaselessness" denotes an unbroken continuation without contemplating interruptions.*

A budget that is people-centric serves as a catalyst for societal security and the comprehensive development of individuals. It is only through the alignment of fiscal policies with the overarching goal of human progress that a budget can truly fulfill its purpose. Pursuits that prioritize material gains over societal welfare, or that are characterized by unrealistic promises and investments, deviate from this essential focus.

To effectively tackle immediate socio-economic challenges and to secure sustainable growth, budgetary planning must transcend short-term fixes and superficial displays of prosperity. A well-conceived budget should prioritize essential societal needs, shed outdated expenditures, and confidently pursue a path that is both prudent and progressive.

[Commentary] The preceding text constitutes the twenty-sixth chapter. This chapter discusses the Way of Heaven.*

Budgeting is an ongoing process, not a static artifact. It evolves in response to challenges, shaping and being shaped by them. Effective budgeting practices become embedded within the fabric of fiscal management, while ineffective ones become sensational news before fading away. Outdated norms are cast aside in favor of innovation.

Yet, sweeping reforms often fail to bear fruit. This is because our desires often outpace our means, and management approaches can be too rigid and hasty, offering little of substance. Consider the typical project budget as a prime example: there's a rush to optimize resource allocation, with excessive and unrealistic demands leading to increased workloads. Budgetary capacity and practical realities are ignored, resulting in haphazard execution.

The budget department finds itself laden with duties, lacking autonomy. Meaningful change unfolds organically, emerging subtly and grounded in empirical reality. Such change is gradual, building upon well-established concepts, mechanisms, systems, methods, and talent. Change takes time, and profound change takes even longer.

Take for example the departmental budget reform initiated in 2000. At that time, a departmental budget was still a novel concept. The single account system, government procurement, comprehensive fund balancing, and non-tax revenue were not widely known.

Two decades on, these concepts have become familiar terms, with some even becoming outdated amidst ongoing reforms. Time is a critical factor in development. Imposing arbitrary timelines for budgetary changes and trying to shortcut history often backfires, leading to suboptimal outcomes.

The budget underpins governance. It addresses two fundamental questions: What does the government do, and how does it do it? The answers to these questions shape the scope and focus of budget allocation and the methods of securing the budget. As the government's boundaries and focus shift, so too must the budget's revenue and expenditure. Technological advancements and market reorganization affect the cost and delivery of public services, necessitating agile budgetary adjustments.

In budgetary matters, politics plays a pivotal role. The vision for the country informs the budget's guiding ideology, principles, ideas, and tasks over the medium to long term. The vision for the government shapes the budget's decision-making process and its revenue and expenditure structure. Major state and government development decisions set the budget's overall direction and thought process.

These elements are the pillars of the budget. Establishing them defines the budget model, and their continuous refinement represents the budget's ongoing evolution.

The outcomes of such an open system are unpredictable, yet this very openness is what allows for adaptability and growth.

Chapter 27
Budget Strategies

[Zhongyong] How great is the Way of the sage!

[Commentary] The forthcoming discourse encompasses the subsequent two sections.*

The budget runs throughout the way of governing the country. Focusing on the crucial part of the country and adhering to basic laws can lead a promising and stable path.

[Zhongyong] Vast and expansive, it cultivates all things, extending up to the sky.

[Commentary] The Way reaches such a lofty domain that nothing else exists beyond its confines.*

The budget permeates all facets of public life. However, it does not serve as a dominator or constraint, but rather, functions as a nurturer and facilitator. It is in the endless flow that the budgets move in cycles and nourish everything.

[Zhongyong] How remarkable it is! It encompasses the three hundred rules of rites, and the three thousand rules of conduct.

[Commentary] This statement implies that the Way permeates into such minute details that one can observe its existence ubiquitously.*

The regulations, systems, institutions, mechanisms, processes, and standards of budgets are not rigid. It is only when the essence of the budgets is invigorated, and this essence is maneuvered appropriately, that the budgets can be well-organized and dynamic. By doing so, the budgets can fulfill their intended role without deviation.

[Zhongyong] It waits for the right followers to carry out.

[Commentary] It encapsulates the preceding two chapters.*

Note: The paragraphs marked with an asterisk (*) are sourced from Zhu Xi's *Sishu Zhangju Jizhu* (Collected Commentaries on the Four Books), specifically *Zhongyong Zhangju* (Commentaries on the Zhongyong), Chapter 27, page 36.

Y. Gou, *The Mean in Budgeting*, https://doi.org/10.1007/978-981-96-9592-8_27

The purpose of budgets is intrinsically human and determined by human agency. The needs, qualities, consciousness, historical context, organizational structures, and modes of interaction of humans fundamentally dictate the characteristics and trajectories of the budget. The unity and diversity inherent in human nature fundamentally determine the unity and diversity of budgets.

[Zhongyong] Hence it is said: "Without the perfection of virtue, the ideal Way cannot be realized."

[Commentary] The content of the ideal Way is mentioned in the preceding two chapters.*

The outcome of budgets is subject to vision of people, and the progression of budgets is contingent upon people. The budgetary efforts, such as listening to the public, understanding the laws governing progress, improving the rules of operation, and enhancing the level of science and technology, can only come to fruition through the improvement of the quality and realm of people.

[Zhongyong] Thus, the Noble Man reveres virtue and pursues knowledge; He expands his understanding and delves into the subtleties; He reaches the heights of wisdom while following the path of moderation. By revisiting the old, he gains new insights. He cultivates a sincere and generous heart, upholding propriety with reverence.

[Commentary] "To revere" means to hold in respectful esteem. "Virtue" refers to the righteous principles I have received from Heaven. Revering virtue involves setting aspirations to reach the highest state of the great Way. Following the Way through learning involves seeking knowledge to understand all the details of the Way. Both are the foundations of cultivating virtue and consolidating the Way. One should not obscure oneself with even the slightest personal will or be burdened by the smallest selfish desire. Repeatedly reflecting on and digesting what one already knows, and further mastering what one can already do, are all part of setting aspirations. Analyzing principles without any bias, handling affairs without errors of excess or deficiency, understanding meanings with daily new insights, and being cautious in behavior where one was previously not careful are all part of seeking knowledge. Generally speaking, without lofty aspirations, there is no motivation to seek knowledge. Once lofty aspirations are set, one must seek knowledge. Therefore, these five sentences complement each other, with the beginning and end echoing each other. The methods of human virtue shown by sages are the most detailed, and learners should wholeheartedly and diligently comprehend them.*

Budgeting represents an unending exploration, serving the public by understanding their needs, delving into the dynamics of progress, venturing into the technological frontiers, and unlocking the potential for resource distribution.

Resilience in budgets involves ensuring stable and dependable revenue streams, channeling resources towards fundamental, significant and long-term domains, and pursuing excellence in spending, allocation norms, execution processes, and evaluation techniques. This ensures that pivotal budgetary decisions and their execution are grounded in a solid microeconomic foundation.

In reality, budgets are rigorously tested. The notion of achieving political success and employing well-designed methods certainly wields influence, but it is the efficacy of measures that truly resonate with people.

Progress in budgets frequently comes through compromise. It is challenging for budgets to shed historical baggage, as addressing present issues frequently requires revisiting and reassessing past choices to pave the way forward.

Returning to their foundational principles is essential for budgets; when consumed by the tumult of reality, they risk losing sight of their core purpose. Realigning with these principles, steadfastly adhering to them, is imperative to navigate back to the ideal path of budgeting.

[Zhongyong] Therefore, he resides in a position of authority without exhibiting arrogance, and dwells in a humble position without demonstrating rebellion. When the kingdom is well-governed, he can rise through his words. Conversely, when the kingdom is ill-governed, he can shield himself through silence. *The Book of Songs* says: "His intelligence and wit served as his safeguard." Does this not echo the same sentiment?

[Commentary] The term "rise" means to rise to take a position of rank. The aforementioned statement is an excerpt from "Odes to the People" within the chapter of "Major Odes of the Kingdom" of *The Book of Songs*.*

Budgets require stability and sustainability, demanding not only a comprehensive understanding of current conditions but also the adoption of pragmatic methods and strategies.

In times of economic upturn, it is vital to focus on key areas and apply targeted efforts to capitalize on developmental opportunities. In contrast, during economic downturns, it is essential to protect the essential interests and prepare for recovery, ensuring the basic well-being of citizens and the continuity of governance.

Governments face distinct fiscal challenges in times of both abundance and adversity: the former calls for restraint against capricious and impulsive spending, while the latter requires careful risk management and forward-looking actions.

[Commentary] The preceding text constitutes the twenty-seventh chapter. This chapter discusses the Way of Man.*

Budgeting is a set of rules guiding the allocation of financial resources. It is responsible for distributing more than one-third of the Gross Domestic Product (GDP) each year, thereby carrying a considerable burden and exerting a profound influence.

Budgetary principles should be founded on a shared vision, adhere to consistent standards despite varied origins, and aim for precise direction, extensive reach, and widespread acknowledgment. Moreover, it is crucial to tailor strategies to local conditions, align with actual circumstances, and pursue equitable distribution, efficient execution, and satisfactory results.

At its core, budgeting is about generating public value through the use of funds. Its goal and methods are centered around the well-being of people. The essence of a people's budget lies in the individuals who shape and implement it, as they create public value and fulfill their own aspirations, epitomizing the ultimate aim of budgeting.

Budget reforms must facilitate personal transformation and the reorganization of how individuals collaborate. To enact such change, four approaches are essential:

1. Commitment to Budgetary Principles: Establishing a shared understanding of budgetary norms, fostering ethical fiscal conduct, and making the entire budgetary process more standardized, systematic, and democratic. In practice, this involves deepening our grasp of these principles, refining and expanding them, and guiding fiscal practices with adaptable rules.
2. Integration into Value Creation: Budgetary principles should be woven into the process of creating public value. Beyond consensus and adherence to fundamental rules, the budget department should aim for excellence in specific fiscal matters, thereby forming a micro-system and cycle that responds to real needs, solidifies budgetary principles, promotes industry-finance integration, optimizes resource allocation, and stimulates the initiative and creativity of all stakeholders.
3. Consensus Building: The political nature of budgeting means that without a collective agreement, even the best rules are ineffective. Political integrity is a prerequisite for a sound budget, and its merits ultimately rest on the consensus of public opinion. A budget that emerges from the people, serves their interests, and is embraced by them can garner consensus and achieve its objectives.
4. Balance between Inheritance or Innovation: Traditional budgeting is steeped in political, economic, social, and cultural legacies. Attempting to revise the budget without addressing these underlying factors is like repackaging old ideas in a new shell, often leading to failure despite initial fanfare. When the context has evolved, clinging to outdated budget models is tantamount to confining new ideas within old frameworks, which stifles innovation with a sense of banality. Change incurs costs, and adherence to the old system offers no escape. The correct course can only be charted by thoroughly examining the intricacies of budgetary evolution and weighing the advantages and disadvantages of change versus stagnation.

Chapter 28
The Era of Budgeting

[Zhongyong] The Master said: "To be ignorant and inclined to act as per one's will; to be of inferior rank and disregard all regulations; to be existing in the present and adhering to the norms of the past; all these will precipitate complications."

[Commentary] The aforementioned statements are utterances of Confucius and are cited by Zisi.*

Budgets vary from time to time and place to place. It is often impractical to anticipate rapid improvements in the budgetary system and capacity by replicating a foreign budgetary model.

Over the past two decades, novel ideas and models such as zero-based budgeting, accrual accounting, and medium-term expenditure planning have come and gone, leaving grassroots workers still grappling with what they are. The reasons are either these concepts are ill-suited to the actual circumstances or lack appropriate timing for implementation.

Historically, the finance department has frequently been the catalyst behind budgetary reforms, systematically formulating reform programs and endeavoring to propel the reform process. However, this represents an asymmetric mission for the finance department, as it is merely one of the participants in the budgetary reform. Effectuating a radical transformation in the existing state of affairs single-handedly is often unfeasible, and excessive scrutiny and evaluation from the financial perspective will inevitably result in deviations.

In practical terms, the framework to ensure the budget department meets its obligations frequently lacks definition. There are numerous constraints, scarce incentives, and insufficient engagement from the legislative department and the public in the reform.

Note: The paragraphs marked with an asterisk (*) are sourced from Zhu Xi's *Sishu Zhangju Jizhu* (Collected Commentaries on the Four Books), specifically *Zhongyong Zhangju* (Commentaries on the Zhongyong), Chapter 28, pages 36–37.

Y. Gou, *The Mean in Budgeting*, https://doi.org/10.1007/978-981-96-9592-8_28

Over time, procedural formalities overshadow the essence of the tasks at hand, and conceptual plans diverge from their execution. This disconnect leads to a counterproductive situation where considerable effort yields minimal outcomes.

[Zhongyong] No one but the Son of Heaven can preside over rituals, make laws, and determine the written scripts.

[Commentary] The subsequent statements are attributed to Zisi. The rites serve as a bridge that unifies all individuals, irrespective of their relationships and social standing.

Managing budgets is a test to humanity. What occurs with or without funds? A minor deviation at the outset may culminate in a total different result, and a slightest change in decision can cause the budget to deviate from fundamental logic and principles, subsequently allowing various interests and powers to intervene in the budgetary process and plunge it into chaos.

Reflecting upon history, the unpredictability of budgets mirrors that of humanity, and budget robustness is precisely manifested in its capacity to return to common sense and the correct path at a lower cost and within a shorter duration following a deviation. The foundation for accurate budgeting not only pertains to institutional arrangements but also involves the consensus of the entire society on budgetary principles and long-term reverence for budgets.

[Zhongyong] Today, carriages have the same axle-widths, documents are written with the same characters, and individuals conform to the same norms of conduct.

[Commentary] The term "today" pertains to the era in which Zisi resided. With carriages maintaining a standard axle-width, documents inscribed with identical characters, and individuals adhering to consistent norms of conduct, the entire world achieves perfect unity.*

Budgeting is predicated on social consensus. Modifications to the budget that echo the perspectives of a minority are likely to confront substantial opposition and may prove challenging to maintain. Conversely, once a shift in social consensus transpires, alterations to the budget will inevitably ensue, sooner or later.

The management of a budget constitutes a decision-making process concerning the allocation and utilization of resources, and in the absence of the requisite consensus, the process of managing budgets will be fraught with contradictions.

[Zhongyong] Even if one holds the position of a king, the absence of virtue precludes the presumption of creating ritual or music. Similarly, possessing virtue, yet not occupying the position of a king, also inhibits the presumption of creating ritual or music.

[Commentary] Zheng Xuan said, "The individual who undertakes the creation of ritual and music must be a sage assuming the sovereignty of the kingdom."*

The budgetary system serves as the governing principle for resource allocation and utilization. Alterations to this system have precipitated adjustments in the pattern of allocation and usage. It is a simple truth that frequent fluctuations in the budgetary system can engender disarray within the resource allocation framework.

Presently, there is a propensity towards adopting expedient measures over long-term planning, and an increased competition for power and resources rather than a commitment to diligent and meticulous work.

Rather than systematically evaluating the merits and demerits of the current system, and continuously filtering out the undesirable, there is a tendency to blindly push for change based on immediate needs without sufficient investigation and demonstration.

This approach risks leading all involved into a prolonged and exhaustive struggle. Consequently, budget reform has increasingly become a matter of handling errands and muddling through.

Despite the proliferation of forms, evaluations, and reports, tangible improvements in budget capacity and quality remain elusive.

[Zhongyong] The Master said: "I can explain the Xia rituals, yet the records from the Qi cannot verify them. I have learned the Yin rituals, and they are still preserved in the Song. I have learned the Zhou rituals, which still remain in practice. I follow the Zhou."

[Commentary] This statement is also a citation from Confucius. Qi refers to a descendent state of the Xia Dynasty. Song refers to a descendent state of the Yin (also known as Shang) Dynasty. Confucius had once acquired and could elucidate the significance of the rituals from the three dynasties of Xia, Yin, and Zhou. Nevertheless, there was nothing to authenticate the Xia rituals. Although the Yin rituals were extant during that period, they did not align with the contemporary laws. Only the Zhou rituals, which had established the ritual system of the king at that time, were adopted. Not holding the position of a king, Confucius adhered to the ritual system of the Zhou Dynasty.*

Each era has its distinctive budget topics and models. Various models such as the itemized budget, performance budget, plan program budget, zero-base budget, and target budget have respectively addressed issues of their times, and have subsequently receded from the historical stage.

Each epoch is confronted with its own pressing issues that necessitate appropriate solutions. While history does not repeat itself, the budgeting concepts and models may still have value. However, mere replication of these models would render them ill-suited to contemporary conditions.

It is imperative to leverage historical experience in light of China's actual circumstances to identify an effective budget model that is firmly rooted in China.

[Commentary] The preceding text constitutes the twenty-eighth chapter. This chapter elucidates the concept of a person abiding in a low position without being rebellious, which is also the Way of Man.*

Budgeting is replete with conflicting elements. For example, the medium-term budget is a commendable concept, yet in the absence of a foundation for revenue forecasting and expenditure planning, its enforcement can be hard with minimal results.

Budget performance management is a promising direction, but it necessitates a comprehensive reform, without which it lacks a robust foundation. The more pressure the finance department exerts on the budget department, the greater the counterforce it will encounter, leading to a game of evasion that is likely to engender more manipulation than performance.

Exploring the various budgeting frameworks and methodologies in the budgetary history might produce some insights. Yet, practitioners often provide evasive responses concerning the objectives of these models, the challenges encountered during their implementation, and the valuable lessons gained from experience, practitioners often provide evasive responses, as evidenced in ambiguous documentation and lackluster reports. Scholars, on the other hand, tend to use theoretical constructs and models to represent reality, converting a process inherently filled with discrepancies and disputes into a coherent and systematic operation.

The initiatives of other nations or regions may seem robust and successful at first glance, yet, a more thorough analysis often reveals that these high-profile projects fail to come to fruition.

Consequently, modern governance should be rooted in the present context, and China's strategies must be in harmony with its actual conditions. This requires a deep reverence for its governance heritage and an extensive grasp of China's governance reality. Given that there are no precedents to follow, we must abandon illusions and, with a pragmatic approach and self-reliance, explore a path of budgeting with Chinese characteristics.

Chapter 29
The Gains and Losses of Budgeting

[Zhongyong] In ruling a state, there are three essentials through which a king can minimize his errors.

[Commentary] Lü Buwei said, "The three essentials can only be executed by the king. The first pertains to presiding over rituals. The second involves the formulation and enactment of laws, standards, and norms. The third encompasses the correction and examination of languages and characters in terms of their script, pronunciation, and expression. With these measures, the country can stabilize its rule, families within the country will adhere to the same customs, and the king will be able to reduce his mistakes."*

Effective governance necessitates proficient management of budgets. Budgets that are uncontrolled, inefficient, and fraught with risk can undermine the bedrock of governance. What budgetary principles and logic should be adhered to in order to circumvent significant errors? The decision makers would surely benefit from a discreet and objective analysis and assessment prior to drawing an ambitious budget.

[Zhongyong] The rituals of those above are excellent, yet unverifiable; thus, trust will not be conferred. In the absence of trust, the people will not follow. The rituals by those below are excellent, yet lower in rank; thus, respect will not be accorded. Without respect, trust will not be established. In the absence of trust, the people will not follow.

[Commentary] The reference to individuals in a position of high rank pertains to previous kings. This accounts for why the ritual systems of the Xia and Shang Dynasties, despite their excellence, cannot be verified. The lack of high rank refers to the situation of the sage. For instance, Confucius, despite his goodness, lacks rank.*

Budgets reflect the will of the people and the government. Communication between the government and the public should remain open and unimpeded. Budgets must fully heed and incorporate the will of the people in the decision-making process,

Note: The paragraphs marked with an asterisk (*) are sourced from Zhu Xi's *Sishu Zhangju Jizhu* (Collected Commentaries on the Four Books), specifically *Zhongyong Zhangju* (Commentaries on the Zhongyong), Chapter 29, pages 37–38.

Y. Gou, *The Mean in Budgeting*, https://doi.org/10.1007/978-981-96-9592-8_29

and secure their understanding and endorsement, thereby laying a foundation for legitimacy and seamless execution.

Within government institutions, communication should also be unobstructed. It is essential to put in place a responsibility mechanism, providing guidance at the macro level, delegating power at the micro level, and by institutionalizing an eco-system that encourages budget departments to innovate, create, and strive for excellence. By doing so, consensus building can take place between different governmental departments and between the people and the government, fiscal funds can be utilized for performance, and the people can be content with the budgets and the government.

[Zhongyong] Therefore, the Way of the Ruler is based on his own character, projected by other people, and compared with the paths of the three preceding sage-kings so he makes no error. The Way is tested by Heaven and Earth so that it is passable, by the spirits of his ancestors so that it is beyond doubt, and by sages of a hundred generations to come so that there is no confusion.

> [Commentary] The Way of the Ruler encompasses the presiding on ritual rules, the formulation and enactment of laws, standards, and norms, as well as the correction and examination of languages and characters in terms of their script, pronunciation, and expression. The initiation of the practice of the Way from oneself signifies the king's virtue. The projection of his character to all the people serves as a method of verifying the thoughts and beliefs of the people. The establishment between Heaven and Earth refers to the king taking action based on the Way and consulting it. The spirits of the ancestors are perceived as a miraculous creation of nature. The anticipation of a sage's appearance over a hundred generations without confusion implies that even if the sage were to resurrect, he would not propose a differing opinion on the king's pronouncements.*

The cornerstone of a budget is the people, with the overarching objective to enhance people's happiness and quality of life. Budgets that do not contribute to human development contravene the fundamental principles of budgeting.

Budgets should fully incorporate the public opinions, empathize with their joys and sorrows, safeguard their basic rights and dignity, and assist them in constructing their self-identity and pursuing a better life.

In addition, budgets must operationalize core political ideologies and governance strategies as efficiently as possible. The efficacy of a budget is a testament to the fulfillment of political objectives, while its shortcomings reflect on the inefficacy of political strategies.

As budgets are pivotal for development, the budget department, when overseeing fiscal management, must merge industrial and financial strategies, ensure that budget planning and execution align with developmental laws, and guarantee seamless practical application across varying scenarios, thus affirming the budget's effectiveness.

The budgetary process should engage in introspection, tracing the roots and trajectories of projects, standards, expenditure ranges, and organizational frameworks, and assess the viability of maintaining established norms or pursuing innovative changes. A thorough and honest review of historical practices is essential to address current challenges with clarity and efficacy.

Above all, budgets must also be forward-looking. The immediate impacts of significant budgetary revenues and expenditures may be ambiguous, often requiring extensive periods to evaluate their true merit. Essentially, a substantial budget is a strategic investment by the government, carrying potential for high returns and risks. Only initiatives that demonstrate enduring value over time should be incorporated into standard budgetary practices.

[Zhongyong] If one can present oneself to the ancestral spirits without harboring any doubts, one knows Heaven. If one can patiently anticipate the emergence of a sage over a span of a hundred generations, one knows human beings.

[Commentary] To know both Heaven and human beings is to know their principles.*

Budgeting is a multifaceted process encompassing actualization, reconciliation, and introspection. It brings public initiatives to fruition, adhering to the operational logic of public affairs. With finite resources and a plethora of needs, budgeting must strategically prioritize and adopt a holistic perspective.

Ideally, the marginal utility of each budget item should be similar, striving for parity. Although excessive comparisons are discouraged, budgeting inherently involves weighing options, and higher aspirations necessitate more extensive evaluations.

The collective aspiration for an improved quality of life finds expression through the budget, necessitating its alignment with the public's sentiment. The budgeting process should be designed to capture the full spectrum of public opinion.

In the face of constrained resources and diverse demands, the budget must serve as a vessel for justice, ensuring equitable consideration of all stakeholders' interests. The preparation and decision-making phases of the budget should facilitate comparative analysis and potential replication.

A budget backed by societal consensus is adaptable; without it, the budget is prone to encounter numerous challenges.

[Zhongyong] Consequently, the conduct of the Ruler will be perceived as the Way for the world. His actions will be perceived as the norm for the world. His words will be perceived as the convention for the world.

[Commentary] In this discussion, "conduct" refers to the words and actions. "The Way" signifies the norm and convention.*

We should reduce mistakes in budgets, using basic budget principles and the law governing development to reassess past budget decisions and budget bases. This involves suspending obsolete and unnecessary revenues and expenditures, eliminating redundancy and complexity, and enhancing management. These principles and laws should also be employed to rigorously evaluate new budget needs, clarify objectives, control costs, and improve management.

Meanwhile, we should establish exit mechanisms to maximize budget allocation and the performance. Given that public resources are susceptible to mismatches and inefficiencies, we should approach budgetary initiatives with extreme caution by reexamining the fundamental questions. Is it necessary to increase taxes? Is it feasible to refrain from increasing spending? Naturally, this logic is applicable mostly to general situations, and an excessive weighing or hesitation in the face of crisis can precipitate serious complications.

[Zhongyong]*The Book of Songs* says: In his absence, he does not incur hatred. In his presence, he does not elicit dislike. In every circumstance, from dawn till dusk, their praise of him is relentless. There has never been a Noble Man who attained rapid recognition from the world and who did not embody these traits.

[Commentary] This excerpt is derived from the section of "White Egrets" within the chapter of "Sacrificial Odes of Zhou" of *The Book of Songs*. It pertains to the six virtues that a gentleman commences with himself in order to manifest his character.*

Budget quality hinges on each aspect of its process. Meticulous preparation enables sound decisions and execution, essential for precise evaluations. The time and effort devoted to budgetary preparation will be manifested in high-quality budget decisions and execution. Continuous refinement throughout the budget cycle ensures correction of planning oversights and decision errors. Rigorous evaluations then inform the next budget cycle, enhancing planning and execution.

Concurrently, issues in any budget cycle can affect others, influencing the overall budget direction. Moreover, to prevent management failures often associated with the overconfidence and inflated self-interest of the participants, rules and institutional frameworks must align the budget with the economy's size, ensure balance, and impose necessary constraints, securing budget stability.

[Commentary] The preceding text constitutes the twenty-ninth chapter. This chapter elucidates the concept of maintaining a position of authority without exhibiting arrogance, which is also synonymous with the Way of Man.

One should not expect budgets to be perfect. A good budget is one with minimal errors. While budget ideals can exist, one should not anticipate ideal budgets. Attractive budgets may lack utility, useful ones may not adhere to regulations, compliant ones may fall short on effectiveness, and effective ones may not gain widespread acceptance.

Budgeting is inherently political, reflecting politicians' visions, public sentiment, and bureaucratic operations. Without political backing, public discourse, and administrative efficiency, even the most vocal declarations cannot materialize a sound budget.

The budget is a blueprint for progress, consistently revealing human potential, adapting to nature, driving innovation, and advancing society. It starts and ends with the people: funded by their contributions and designed for their needs. This collaborative process reflects culture, resources, technology, and governance. Learning from the past, setting realistic goals, and efficiently managing revenue, allocation, and redistribution are pivotal for achieving future aspirations.

The budget's role in reallocating resources enables individual and collective growth. It presents both prospects and pitfalls.

Passive acceptance or silence means forfeiting the right to influence public resource distribution. Without sound decision-making, societal misconceptions can arise, transforming the government into a Leviathan and converting the budget into a catalyst for economic recession, social stratification, and cultural deterioration.

Quality budgets are rare; bad budgets are common. Those involved in budgeting must have a sense of vigilance: to respect nature, to respect society, to respect technology, and to maintain an attitude of humility and self-reflection. Diligent oversight and committed effort are essential to prevent exhaustive processes from yielding disappointing results.

Chapter 30
The Politics of Budgeting

[Zhongyong] Confucius transmitted the legacy of the sage-kings Yao and Shun and fashioned his character in the likeness of the sage-kings Wen and Wu. He was governed by the Heavenly seasons from above and combined the elements of Earth and Waters below.

[Commentary] Individuals who perpetuated the legacy of sage-kings inherited the ethics and wisdom of their forebears. Those who modeled their character on that of sage-kings adhered to the character of sage-kings. Individuals who were governed by the Heavenly seasons adhered to the laws of nature. Those who were governed by the Earth and Waters adhered to the constraints of natural conditions. All these elements should be harmonized both internally and externally, taking into account both major and minor aspects.*

Budgets should be guided by ideals. The budget ideal is subordinate to the national ideal, serving the national ideal and illuminating the path towards the reality of budgets. Budgets strategies form an integral part of the national strategy.

As we transition into a new stage of development, budgeting should adhere to the new development philosophy and foster a new development paradigm by modernizing the budget system and enhancing budgeting capabilities.

Budgets should reflect its times. Based on the internal and external context of China's development and China's economic realities, budgeting should adhere to political ideals, solidify the foundation of budgets, and advance development of all endeavors.

Budgets should also reflect national characteristics. Rooted in China's reality, budgeting should align with Chinese cultural traditions, habits, and the needs of the Chinese people, and adapt to China's political system and governance methods. This approach can effectively address the practical problems of government budgets at all levels.

Note: The paragraphs marked with an asterisk (*) are sourced from Zhu Xi's *Sishu Zhangju Jizhu* (Collected Commentaries on the Four Books), specifically *Zhongyong Zhangju* (Commentaries on the Zhongyong), Chapter 30, page 38.

Y. Gou, *The Mean in Budgeting*, https://doi.org/10.1007/978-981-96-9592-8_30

[Zhongyong] His virtue was akin to that of Heaven and Earth, which offer unwavering support and encompass all things. His function mirrored the cyclical revolution of the four seasons and the alternating transition of the sun and moon.

[Commentary] This chapter discusses the virtue of the perfect sage.*

For the government, budgets are omnipresent. Only through comprehensive budget management can resources be systematically allocated, management be standardized, and risks be controlled.

Budgets evolve persistently, demanding that regulations adapt to governance needs. Some budgets are ensured while others are cut. It's through this relentless progression that financial and administrative integration is achieved.

[Zhongyong] He nurtures the myriad entities, and they mature together without causing harm to one another, and they pursue their respective paths concurrently without mutual interference. His lesser power is akin to the rivers and streams. His greater power is manifested in profound transformations. This is the reason why Heaven and Earth are referred to as "great".

[Commentary] Heaven envelops everything, and Earth sustains everything. Within the realm of Heaven and Earth, myriad entities are nurtured and mature without causing harm to one another. The Sun and Moon traverse their respective paths without mutual interference. Not causing harm or interference constitutes lesser power, comparable to rivers and streams. Nurturing and maturing concurrently constitutes great power, which is evident in the profound transformation of everything. Lesser power refers to the part of a whole. Greater power refers to the essence of all entities. This passage discusses the Way of Heaven and Earth, which aligns with the discourse in the preceding paragraph.*

Optimal budget management ensures sectoral harmony and governmental accountability, with each entity performing its role without overstepping.

Taxation should be fair, without redundancy or excess, and adherence to regulations is paramount. In case of discrepancies, corrective fiscal policies must be applied, including tax exemptions, reductions, and strict collection.

Project spending and market operations should be streamlined to avoid overlap and conflict. If competition is counterproductive, consolidation and realignment of plans, functions, and fiscal relations are necessary.

When making budgetary preparation, one must always consider its alignment with objectives, resource efficiency, and project support.

Ultimately, every fiscal decision should be gauged by its contribution to societal well-being and the potential for better resource utilization. Budgets must remain dynamic, evolving with time to sustain their relevance and effectiveness.

[Commentary] The preceding text constitutes the thirtieth chapter. This chapter discusses the Way of Heaven.*

Budgets are tools for realizing political visions. They draw inspiration from the ideal of harmonious governance, akin to the natural order of heaven and earth.

"The ruler must contemplate the means of pacifying the world, and the minister should act in harmony with Heaven and Earth; only thus be apt to govern the people."

This ideal, though elusive, gives purpose to the meticulous crafting of financial documents, like endless reports, tables, figures, and exhaustive budgetary exercises. It also functions as a yardstick for evaluating budgetary processes.

Budget frameworks are not created in a vacuum; they must align with governance strategies and fiscal realities. They evolve, blending old wisdom with new insights, all in pursuit of these guiding principles. Without them, budgetary efforts lack direction.

Nevertheless, if we adhere to the political or budgetary ideals regardless of the situation and reality, we will diverge significantly from our objectives.

Pragmatism is key; ideals must be balanced with fiscal prudence. Tax adjustments, spending allocations, and management mechanisms must reflect the current economic context and budgetary reality. In tough economic times, budgets must prioritize public welfare and invigorate the community. When economic and social contradictions are prominent, budget architects must navigate challenges, drawing on established fiscal principles while eschewing outdated practices.

A budget grounded in reality, yet rejuvenated with innovative approaches, ensures its efficacy and relevance.

Budgets permeate all aspects of fiscal planning, not in the sense of pepper sprinkles, but in the sense of adopting a comprehensive and inclusive perspective on budgetary administration.

Within the domain of budgets, there should be justifications for ensuring expenditures and reasons for not doing so. What is guaranteed presently may gradually vanish, and what is not guaranteed now may emerge as a future expenditure focus.

Time passes unceasingly. Budgets continually evolve in an eternal cycle of change. Just when one believes they have a thorough understanding, its behavior yields surprises.

Budgets are annual, with a distinct commencement and conclusion. The burden of income tasks and expenditure responsibilities can be daunting. Yet, budgets are also cyclical, devoid of visible boundaries.

Effective budgeting hinges on foresight and strategic planning. Without a medium to long-term outlook, and proactive measures, fiscal governance becomes untenable. Immediate challenges arise from a lack of preparation. The long-term consequences of specific revenues and expenditures must be assessed against the backdrop of broader economic and social progress, within the dynamic stream of budgetary flows.

Budgeting can range from the simple income collection and expenditure allocation to a level of complexity where multiple income sources and expenditures interweave into a dense network that encompasses the entire resource allocation of the government and society.

From a macroscopic perspective, income and expenses must be balanced and sustainable, bolstering the efficient operation of the governance system, fostering governance capabilities, and assisting in the execution of governance strategies.

From a microscopic perspective, the purpose of every income source must be identified, and every expenditure must trace its origin.

The crux of overlapping and conflicting budgets lies in inefficient governmental operation. To optimize the budget, it is imperative to adjust the governance mode and structure.

Budgets do not improve autonomously. Political or budgetary ideals guide budgetary reforms. Resolving minor issues within the budget will not engender substantial changes in the budgetary field.

Budgetary transformations stem from breakthroughs in understanding and practice concerning a series of major issues, such as economics and society, government and market, central and local, domestic and international, and consumption and construction.

Chapter 31
The Framework of Budgeting

[Zhongyong] Only the perfect sage possesses the requisite acumen, sharpness, and insight to govern all. In addition, he possesses sufficient generosity, open-mindedness, warmth, and flexibility to embrace all. He possesses ample energy, strength, firmness, and determination to preserve what he has. He possesses sufficient self-awareness, solemnity, centeredness, and correctness to command respect. He possesses enough culture, analytical ability, depth, and discernment to discriminate.

[Commentary] The acumen, sharpness, and insight are the natural aptitudes of the sage. The subsequent four aspects of the characteristics of the perfect sage correspond to the virtues of benevolence, righteousness, propriety, and wisdom. *

Budgeting and planning are intertwined, necessitating that budgetary frameworks be developed in harmony with societal goals. The establishment of a multi-year budget framework allows for the strategic allocation of resources and annual adjustments to the budget structure, reflecting the evolving needs of societal development and the nation's actual capabilities. To align with China's governance traditions and practical realities, we should follow the following principles in budgeting.

1. Humanistic Budgeting: The budget formulation must reflect humanistic values, ensuring provision of essential public services, protection of fundamental rights to subsistence and development, support for rural revitalization, and promotion of inclusive growth.
2. Prioritization of Key Areas: Budget allocation should focus on major tasks to leverage strategic advantages, and address critical issues and remove obstacles impeding long-term progress.

Note: The paragraphs marked with an asterisk (*) are sourced from Zhu Xi's *Sishu Zhangju Jizhu* (Collected Commentaries on the Four Books), specifically *Zhongyong Zhangju* (Commentaries on the Zhongyong), Chapter 31, pages 38–39.

Y. Gou, *The Mean in Budgeting*, https://doi.org/10.1007/978-981-96-9592-8_31

3. Disciplined Execution: Budget execution requires strict adherence to the Budget Law and its regulations, lawful and regulation-compliant governance, and utilization of the budget as a tool for government modernization.
4. Strengthening Foundations: To solidify the budget's role, it is essential to enhance budget management efficiency, deepen budget performance management, ensure budget departments fulfill their primary responsibilities, and establish a lean administration with transparent incentives and accountability.

[Zhongyong] Immeasurably expansive and profoundly deep, the sage utilizes his abilities in accordance with the circumstances.

[Commentary] All the aforementioned five virtues reside within the heart of the perfect sage himself and can be enacted in alignment with time and situation. *

Budget adapts to the times. Consequently, budgets necessitate control, planning, or administration. The emphasis on certain functions does not preclude the existence of other functions.

Without control, how can we devise plans to manage the budgets? Without planning, how can we administer the budgets? In the absence of administration, how can we attain control?

Budgets are expansive and profound, and only through comprehending the entirety can we understand the constituent parts.

Budgeting evolves with time, requiring a balance of control, planning, and administration, each element being crucial. These functions are interdependent - control validates plans, planning guides administration, and administration enforces control.

Grasping the whole concept is key to understanding its parts, ensuring a holistic fiscal approach.

[Zhongyong] As expansive as the heavens and as profound as an abyss, when he shows himself, there are none who do not revere him. When he speaks, there are none who do not trust him. When he acts, there are none who do not value him.

[Commentary] The virtues of the perfect sage are plentiful, and the enactment of these virtues is powerful. *

Effective budgeting embodies is the government's a pledge to its citizens. Budgets that are forward-looking, pragmatic, unambiguously defined, and transparent can garner the trust and support of the people if implemented proficiently.

[Zhongyong] Consequently, his name resonates from the central kingdoms to the uncivilized regions. Wherever boats and wagons traverse, wherever human power extends; in every locale supported by the Earth; those places bathed in the light of the sun and moon; wherever dew and frost descend; wherever beings draw breath, there are none who do not revere and cherish him. Therefore, he is associated with Heaven.

[Commentary] By invoking imagery of boats and wagons and subsequent elements, the discourse underscores the magnitude of the influence of the perfect sage. By associating the perfect sage with Heaven, it conveys the notion that the virtues of the perfect sage pervade the world akin to the expansiveness of Heaven. *

Budgeting has a bearing on a nation's international standing. A budget that garners wide public acceptance can foster national development and augment the well-being of the citizenry, thereby elevating the nation's stature within the global community. Furthermore, the effective utilization of international expenditures within the budget can enhance China's international influence.

[Commentary] The preceding text constitutes the thirty-first chapter. In continuation of the preceding chapter, this chapter delves into the discourse on minor virtues, which also pertains to the Way of Heaven. *

How does one achieve an ideal budget? There are at least five requirements:

1. Meticulous Consideration. The budget is both an investment and an innovative creation. Only through meticulous considerations can we identify the real needs and devise effective solutions to address urgent requirements and achieve long-term benefits.
2. Tolerance. Budgeting encompasses the entire society and all beings. Individuals from all industries, classes, nationalities, and regions, as well as society and nature, should coexist and prosper together. The budget should be broad-minded and people-oriented to promote inclusive development.
3. Firmness. Budgets can easily spiral out of control in the face of numerous temptations. In the face of the temptation to increase government revenue without limit, we should be cognizant of the potential failure and employ procedures and rules to control its scale. In the face of the temptation of unlimited expenditure needs, power-related projects, and image projects, we should implement the governance strategy and avoid straying from the main line.
4. Prudence. The budget is perpetually one step away from the abyss, with the process fraught with risks. On a macro level, financial risks should be controlled, methods should be identified to reveal financial risks, and the scale of debt should be strictly controlled within the government's capability. On a micro level, internal control mechanisms should be consistently improved to avoid compliance risks.
5. Optimization. With ambitious individuals and government, there exists a standardized and efficient budget. Each link of the budget cycle should be permeated with ambitious thinking. By implementing clear and concrete regulations as well as effective execution, the budget may exhibit commendable performance.

Ideal budgets should be comprehensive and profound. Comprehensiveness implies a focus on expenditure, long-term planning, and inclusivity. Profundity suggests a robust economic foundation for revenue that is stable, sufficient, and continuously sourced.

Ideal budgets should also adhere to the principle of the mean by aligning with the laws of economic, political, cultural, social, and ecological development.

By not shying away from challenges, avoiding superficial indicators, and refraining from giving up, and by setting objectives, devising measures, and nurturing the ability to implement decisions, the budgets will prove beneficial to the people, garnering widespread recognition and respect from both the people and the government, and serving as a predictable, feasible, and satisfactory method of budgeting.

With ideal budgets, we can secure a respected, convincing, and satisfied government and people, and can thus fulfill responsibilities and function internationally with due diligence, winning widespread respect, trust, and satisfaction.

Chapter 32
The Government in Budgeting

[Zhongyong] Only the individuals with perfect sincerity can adjust the threads on the great loom of the world, set the great root of the world, and to comprehend the transformations and the nurturing of Heaven and Earth. What else can he rely on other than sincerity?

[Commentary] The threads on the great loom of the world refer to the fundamental five relations of the people, namely, the relation between father and son, king and minister, husband and wife, elder brother and younger brother, and the relation between friends. The great root of the world refers to the entirety of one' nature. The virtue of the perfect sage is so sincere, devoid of any selfishness and hypocrisy, that the basic five relations of the people can be fulfilled, which serves as the model for the later generations. In the entirety of one's nature, there is not the slightest trace of selfish desires or falsehood. The myriad transformations of the Way in the world all originate from this point, which is referred to as "setting the great root". His extreme sincerity and unwavering heart resonate with the creation and nurturing of Heaven and Earth, not merely through sensory knowledge. These are the natural effects of utmost sincerity and truthfulness, not dependent on external things to be achieved. *

The budget model cannot be replicated. The nature of our government dictates the type of budget we have. Only a government that truly represents its people can establish a budget that is people-centric, coordinates resources from diverse channels, optimizes allocation towards the great causes of the nation, and fosters the comprehensive development of all sectors.

The essence of the budget lies in politics. Only when politics are sound can the budget be sound, and only when politics are progressive can the budget be progressive. While the budget system and management are crucial, adhering to the correct political direction is essential for the budget to have a promising future.

Note: The paragraphs marked with an asterisk (*) are sourced from Zhu Xi's *Sishu Zhangju Jizhu* (Collected Commentaries on the Four Books), specifically *Zhongyong Zhangju* (Commentaries on the Zhongyong), Chapter 32, page 39–40.

Y. Gou, *The Mean in Budgeting*, https://doi.org/10.1007/978-981-96-9592-8_32

[Zhongyong] His benevolence is so earnest; his depth is unfathomable; his vastness is sky-bound.

[Commentary] Earnestness is the manner in which an individual adjusts the threads on the great loom of the world. Depth pertains to the great root of the world. Vastness refers to the immensity of the gentleman's comprehension of the transformative and the nurturing nature of Heaven and Earth. The comprehension does not merely resemble the depth of the abyss and the vastness of the sky. Rather, it is the very embodiment of the abyss and the sky itself. *

The ideal state of budgets embodies three distinct characteristics. Firstly, it is people-oriented, seeking and striving for an enhanced quality of life predicated on the aspirations of the people, as well as fostering innovation and excellence.

Secondly, budgets should possess a robust foundation. Financial resources should be earnestly cultivated, and fiscal risks should be judiciously managed. Budget arrangements should be rooted in practicality, and budget execution should be oriented towards achieving tangible results.

Lastly, budget management should encompass a broad vision. The new development philosophy should be embodied, national strategies should be implemented, thereby promoting comprehensive human development.

[Zhongyong] Only those who possess acumen and wisdom—who are imbued with heavenly virtue can understand them.

[Commentary] Zheng Xuan said: "Only sages can understand sages." *

The budget ideal is the result of a government that is ambitious, enterprising, and committed to perpetual improvement.

[Commentary] The preceding text constitutes the thirty-second chapter. This chapter builds upon the preceding one and discusses the profound transformations observed in great power, which is the Way of Heaven. The previous chapter delved into the virtues of the perfect sage. This chapter explores the concept of perfect sincerity. However, only the perfect sage can comprehend perfect sincerity. Without sincerity, the virtue of the perfect sage cannot be realized. Therefore, these two elements cannot be considered in isolation. This chapter pertains to the zenith of the sage and the Way of Heaven, and nothing can augment this extreme. *

Through resource allocation, the budget mirrors the government's intentions, rectifies market failures, and fosters the development and harmony among individuals, society, and nature. The orchestration and decision-making of budget revenues and expenditures rest with the budget makers.

If these individuals solely pursue personal interests and gains and losses, the budget process cannot effectively curb political favoritism or reconcile conflicting interests. As a result, the budget will fail to execute political strategies and may even engender conflicts and problems.

On the other hand, if the budget makers are dedicated to the public good and sincere in their service to the people, society, and nature, and if the budgeting process is democratic and efficient, the budget is well positioned to respond to public sentiment, serve people's wellbeing, and promote harmonious development in China.

The budget makers and the budget process determine the caliber of the budget. The key factors for success are not technical means, specific management processes, or normative standards, but rather the presence of budget makers imbued with a public spirit and institutional arrangements that foster it.

When politicians with substantial budgetary power commit to public service, budget officials execute their responsibilities with diligence, and citizens engage proactively, the efficacy and reliability of budget performance are significantly bolstered.

Chapter 33
The Vision of Budgeting

[Zhongyong] *The Book of Songs* says: "She enveloped her brocade gown with a modest robe." She refrained from flaunting her finery. Consequently, the Noble Man conducts himself in a manner such that he remains concealed, yet each day accrues luminosity. The petty man reveals himself and each day diminishes in luminosity. The Way of the Noble Man is devoid of flavor, yet one never tires of it. It is simple, yet refined; warm-hearted, yet principled. He comprehends the proximity of the distant, understands the source of the wind. He discerns the manifestation of the subtle and can immerse himself in virtue.

[Commentary] The preceding chapter delves into the virtues of the perfect sage, which is elucidated so comprehensively that nothing necessitates further addition. This chapter commences by discussing the gentleman's virtue of learning from below and making determination, and the subsequent text escalate it to the utmost. The gentleman engages in self-cultivation; thus he is determined. He attempts to conceal himself, yet each day he gains luminosity. The tastelessness, simplicity, and warm-heartedness of the gentleman are akin to the plain robe he dons externally. The engaging, refined, and principled nature of the gentleman resembles the brocade gown he wears internally. In contrast, the petty man consistently focuses on displaying his finery, yet he loses luminosity daily without any substantial elements to support this finery. The proximity of the distant signifies that what originates from afar is actually derived from things nearby. The source of wind implies that what is manifested externally is actually established internally. The manifestation of the subtle signifies that what emanates from within will be revealed outside. By self-cultivation and understanding the aforementioned three elements, an individual will be able to discern what to be cautious about and how to immerse himself in virtue. This is the rationale for the subsequent text discussing the matter of being cautious when alone with the citations from *The Book of Songs*. *

Budgetary practices should be pragmatic and grounded in reality. Grandiose budget reforms often fail to achieve their intended outcomes as they can become

Note: The paragraphs marked with an asterisk (*) are sourced from Zhu Xi's *Sishu Zhangju Jizhu* (Collected Commentaries on the Four Books), specifically *Zhongyong Zhangju* (Commentaries on the Zhongyong), Chapter 33, pages 40–41.

Y. Gou, *The Mean in Budgeting*, https://doi.org/10.1007/978-981-96-9592-8_33

disconnected from reality. The more ostentatious the slogans and promises made during the budget management process, the more challenging it becomes to fully implement the budget. Attractive budget commitments often cannot be fulfilled without a sustainable and stable financial foundation. Regardless of the extent of the rhetoric, any efforts would ultimately be futile without concrete action.

Massive infrastructure projects often quietly conceal fiscal risks, leaving the debt burden to future generations. While this may appear convenient in the short term, such pursuits of short-term political effects or illusory prosperity are challenging to address in the long term and can engender negative consequences. Therefore, the budget cannot function effectively in isolation; it must be positioned within the framework of governance reform.

As the budget cycle recurs, it is crucial to plan for potential changes in the long term. Starting from the reality of the budget, one must assess various internal and external factors. The optimal strategy often exacerbates conflicts and increases costs in the short term without yielding significant immediate results. However, persisting with this approach may improve the budget system and enhance budget capabilities.

To enhance the effectiveness of budget performance management, it is essential to address the core issues, like what needs to be changed, or methods to effect change, rather than peripheral ones. Directly tackling challenges is the key to true progress. Overcoming these bottlenecks demands political bravery and discernment. It is imperative to create enduring mechanisms that drive ongoing improvements at all levels of management.

Currently, the emphasis in budget performance management is on defining clear performance objectives, fortifying cost accounting practices, and crafting robust evaluation systems. While these are foundational, the crux of advancing budget performance management lies in stimulating the drive and innovation of budgetary departments.

This encourages proactive behavior and cultivates a dynamic environment for growth. Such progress transcends budgetary concerns alone, requiring a systematic approach and holistic advancement in the context of establishing a government that values performance. This shift will lead to significant reforms in departmental evaluations, compensation structures, and other related areas.

[Zhongyong] *The Book of Songs* says: "Though the fish descend to the depths, they remain visible." Consequently, the Noble Man, finding no perversity within himself, harbors no malevolent intentions. The very things that the Noble Man is incapable of attaining are precisely the things that others fail to perceive.

[Commentary] This poem is cited from the section "The First Month" within the chapter of "Minor Odes" of *The Book of Songs*, which aligns with the preceding text: "Nothing is more conspicuous than that which is hidden, and nothing is more evident than the subtle." "Harboring no malevolent intentions" refers to possessing a clear conscience. This encapsulates how the gentleman exercises caution when alone. *

The success or failure of budgetary practices is contingent upon the individuals who manage the funds. The numerical data and succinct explanations in a budget proposal merely provide a snapshot of the overall scenario, leaving an indistinct impression. The true complexities are comprehended solely by those with firsthand experience in managing finances.

For budgets to be efficacious, it is imperative that those tasked with managing the funds do so with sincerity, executing the budgets with diligence and exercising prudence in risk control. In reality, budgeting often devolves into a game of evasion. During the budgeting process, insincere proposals may be proffered, tailored to personal predilections or inflated in their assertions.

During budget implementation, a dichotomy between financial and operational concerns can emerge, prioritizing expenditure without adequate planning or flexibility. If those responsible for managing the funds fail to scrutinize expenses meticulously, maintaining control over the budget becomes challenging. Similarly, if they adopt a laissez-faire attitude towards expenditure, the budget will lack proper planning. Furthermore, if they adhere to antiquated practices, the budget will fail to yield the desired outcomes.

A budget mechanism that fosters introspection, self-discipline, and self-improvement among those handling the funds is essential for its effectiveness. Without delving into these aspects and exerting sustained influence, it is challenging to achieve tangible results with budgetary measures.

[Zhongyong] *The Book of Songs* says: "While in your own room, you should not feel embarrassment if it were opened to the world." Consequently, the Noble Man does not act, yet commands respect. He does not utter a word, yet inspires belief.

> [Commentary] This poem is cited from the section "Kingdom Yi" within the chapter of "Major Odes" of *The Book of Songs*, which aligns with the preceding discussion on the sincerity inherent in the self-cultivation of the gentleman. This process is ceaseless. Being respectful and believing prior to taking action or speaking enhances the gentleman's capacity for self-cultivation. This is the rationale for the subsequent text discussing its effect by citing *The Book of Songs*. *

Budget transparency is revolutionizing the budgetary ecosystem. In the era of the internet, the degree of budget transparency has significantly escalated, and advanced methodologies have disseminated rapidly. Participants in the budgetary process must expedite their learning to remain abreast of these trends. Shortcomings and errors are thoroughly exposed, imposing substantial pressure on those accountable.

Enhancing transparency in budgeting reduces obscurity and promotes public oversight, which in turn lessens information asymmetry and heightens the potential for conflict resolution. To refine budgetary rules effectively, it is crucial to:

1. implement performance-oriented mechanisms that drive efficiency, along with the incorporation of competitive mechanisms and incentive structures.
2. define clear financial boundaries, eliminating unnecessary restrictions, and ensuring adherence to well-defined rules and standards. Participants in the budgetary process should not only embrace innovation and pursue excellence, but also adhere strictly to regulations and govern within the bounds of the law.

[Zhongyong] *The Book of Songs* says: "Make your offerings without uttering words, and there will never ensue any disagreement." Consequently, the Noble

Man receives no accolades, yet the people elevates him. He does not exhibit anger, yet they harbor more reverence for him than they do for lethal weapons."

> [Commentary] This poem is cited from the section "Illustrious Ancestor" within the chapter of "Sacrificial Odes of Shang" of *The Book of Songs*, which aligns with the preceding discussion and further elaborates on the impact of the gentleman's capacity for self-cultivation. This section discusses the individual perceives and understands Heaven with pure sincerity. In utmost sincerity and reverence, this individual does not need to articulate any words, yet he is self-transformed. *

The influence of budget culture is profound and far-reaching. Budget systems are indispensable as they provide a framework and orderliness. However, it is crucial to acknowledge that these systems are not panaceas for all challenges.

In regions where the budget system is not implemented, there is frequently a disarray in revenue and expenditures, resulting in drawn-out disputes and squandering of valuable resources. While broadening the scope of the system can mitigate these issues, over-regulation and meticulous rules can also create complications by prioritizing compliance over effectiveness.

This is where culture steps in to bridge the gaps. Participants in the budget process should aim for consensus, implicitly understanding and respecting the fundamental principles, norms, and conventional practices, while acknowledging their constraints. The formation of budget culture requires a gradual process, but once established, it plays a pivotal role.

A culture centered on budget performance can stimulate innovation within budget departments, while a culture grounded in the rule of law can deter infractions. Ultimately, the potency of culture resides in individual cognizance. When participants in the budget process attain a collective comprehension of budget concepts, principles, procedures, and methods, the budget will transition into a new phase.

[Zhongyong] *The Book of Songs* says: "Only by not displaying it can one cultivate virtue. All the princes are bound by this. Hence, the Noble Man, through his magnanimity and decorum, pacifies the realm."

> [Commentary] This passage is cited from the section "Illustrious Virtue" within the chapter of "Sacrificial Odes of Zhou" of *The Book of Songs*. The concept of not displaying virtue is discussed in chapter twenty-six, which alludes to the king's virtue being profound yet inconspicuous. The king possesses virtue but does not display it overtly, yet all the princes are bound by it and adhere to it, resulting in the impact of the virtue being more profound and enduring. Pacifying the world with the king's magnanimity and decorum reflects the supreme and profound virtue of the sage, the response of nature, and the potent effect of the mean. *

The merit of budgets is rooted in their authenticity and rationality. The budgeting procedure has been traditionally perceived as a contested arena for resources, with budget departments endeavoring to secure an upper hand. Requests for funding are frequently inflated, poised for reduction, or intentionally underestimated to accommodate subsequent augmentations. Some resort to innovative and captivating strategies, while others employ scare tactics to garner attention. This spectrum of budget strategies skews budgetary conduct and results in resource misallocation and inefficient fund utilization.

The underlying causes can be traced back to a budget culture within and beyond the government that either prioritizes accomplishments without contemplating repercussions or succumbs to indifference and vacuity. Budget requests lack defined limits, and interdepartmental trust is deficient.

To rectify these issues and realign budgeting with its intended trajectory, it is imperative to institute incentive and deterrent mechanisms that inspire budget participants to remain faithful to the cause and respect the budget, thereby cultivating a budget culture that esteems truth and rationality.

[Zhongyong] ***The Book of Songs*** **says: "I value radiant virtue, not loud noises and ostentatious colors." The Master said: "In the context of transforming individuals, sounds and colors hold minimal significance."** ***The Book of Songs*** **further states: "Virtue is as light as a strand of hair, yet even a strand of hair embodies the grand principles. In the operations of the Supreme Heaven, there is neither sound nor scent. It is perfect."**

[Commentary] This segment is extracted from the section "Kingdom·Huang Yi" within the chapter of "Major Odes" of *The Book of Songs* to illustrate the virtue of not displaying mentioned in the preceding chapter that influences without loud noises and ostentatious colors. Subsequently, the words of Confucius are quoted to underscore that sounds and colors are of least importance in terms of transforming individuals. Therefore, no loud sounds and colors still do not sufficiently convey the virtue of not displaying. The metaphorical expression in the section "Odes to the People" within the chapter of "Major Odes" of *The Book of Songs*: "Virtue is as light as a hair" is more apt. Nonetheless, by using a strand of hair to symbolize the subtle virtue, there remains scope for comparison, thus not utmost subtle virtue. King Wen proclaimed in his poem: "In the functions of Supreme Heaven, there are no sounds or scent." This metaphorical expression can be perceived as the optimal way to illustrate virtue. Sound and scent are subtle entities that exist in gaseous form without any tangible shape. Thus, the absence of sound and scent can express the subtlety of utmost courtesy. Of the three portrayals of virtue, the truly perfect is that which is profoundly subtle, with no sound or scent. *

Managing budgets is about self-improvement. As the budget system evolves, an increasing number of regulations are instituted, which curtail liberty and augment the load on departments, culminating in a surge of grievances. The individuals who expend the funds dictate the triumph or failure of the budget. Appeals will prove futile in the face of the budget department's indifference.

The awakening of the budget department signifies the awakening of the budget itself, and the rationality and freedom of the budget department are indicative of those of the budget. For budgeting, perpetual self-improvement is a defining characteristic, and the ideal state is to silently nurture things and allow nature to take its course.

[Commentary] The preceding text constitutes the thirty-third chapter. Building on the foundation laid in the previous chapter, Zisi explores the fundamental principles and expands on concepts such as "learning from below", "self-cultivation", and "'being cautious when alone", to illustrate the grand state of "pacifying the realm through his magnanimity and decorum". He praises the mystical nature of utmost sincerity, concluding with "neither sound nor scent" to summarize the essence of the entire text. The repeated exhortations and teachings reflect a profound dedication, urging learners to be fully committed. How can one not be wholehearted in their pursuit? *

The advent of the internet era has revolutionized the world of budgeting. The transparency of budgets has seen significant enhancement, with a swift escalation in the accessibility of public information pertaining to budget formulation, decision-making, execution, evaluation, and auditing. The information chasm between government departments, the government and the market, and society is contracting and becoming less profound.

Budgets have now become more comprehensible but also more challenging to manage. As collaborations between the government-market and government-society intensify, and as budget performance management progresses, the market and society are gaining increased cognizance of budgeting and acquiring greater influence and decision-making power.

The jurisdiction of budgets is extending beyond the government, and the organizational structure of budgets is becoming more intricate. With rapidly evolving mindsets, expedited economic and social transformations, the deepening of e-government, and the widespread deployment of technologies such as big data, all budget revenues and expenditures may be subjected to a reevaluation of their value.

Participants in the budget may encounter scrutiny from both within and outside the government at any juncture, and the costs associated with budgetary mismanagement and infractions are on the rise.

What is the trajectory of the future of budgeting?

"Here with this long plough, farmers cultivate lands on the south. This farming products can be shared throughout the country."—from "The Temple and Fields Ode", a pre-Qin text (Qin Dynasty, 221-206BCE). To ensure a sustainable future for generations to come, the Way of budgeting demands that we create and execute budgets that prioritize the well-being of the people, foster awareness of potential risks, encourage continuous self-improvement, and strike a balanced focus on both control and performance.

Budgeting serves the people. When the needs of the people metamorphose into aspirations for an improved quality of life, the structure and priorities of the budget must undergo corresponding alterations.

Taxation or fees ought to be regulated or diminished, bestowing upon the people greater economic autonomy while bolstering economic development. Expenditures should epitomize fairness and justice, with a further enhancement of basic public services. Endeavors should be concentrated on rectifying regional disparities, urban–rural gaps, income inequality, and augmenting the public sense of accomplishment, contentment, and security.

Government budget revenues and expenditures should be open, transparent, comprehensible, and accountable. Major government budget arrangements and adjustments should thoroughly reflect public opinion, ensuring that the budget originates from the people and is in service of the people.

In the face of unparalleled challenges, budgets must aspire for self-sufficiency and resilience. Budgeting must address macroeconomic fiscal risks and elucidate the rules and strategies to ensure medium- and long-term fiscal stability, and prioritize and make choices. Achieving budget equilibrium necessitates proactive responses to unprecedented internal and external risks.

Budget architects need to strive for risk prevention, bear in mind the red lines, ensure proactive and cautious revenue projections, and take into consideration of all factors including budget capacity, various risks and vulnerabilities in economic, political, and social development when orchestrating expenditures.

To foster high-quality development, taxes and fees should be curtailed to stimulate the growth of market entities and the real economy. Meanwhile, robust supports are requisite for technological innovation to secure long-term competitive advantages by planning and envisioning the future.

Fiscal expenditure arrangements should strike a balance between steadfastness and flexibility. While ensuring investment in basic public services, significant efforts should be directed towards enhancing the precision and flexibility of budgetary expenditures, mitigating rigid expenditures, and maximizing the utilization of existing resources. This, in turn, entails circumventing both idle and insufficient situations, and ultimately augmenting the efficiency of budget allocation and fund utilization.

Budget control is a fundamental aspect of government operations, yet the ultimate goal of budgeting extends beyond control to enhancing performance.

Traditionally, budget control preceded performance improvement, or performance was improved by relaxing control measures. Today, our collective mission is to simultaneously strengthen control and boost performance, presenting a significant challenge.

The path forward lies in the innovative transformation of the budget governance model, guided by a new developmental paradigm. This involves establishing a medium-term budget framework that aligns with national strategies and budgets, clarifying objectives, maintaining momentum, and mitigating systemic risks.

Additionally, it's crucial to adopt a comprehensive approach to budget performance management, understand the mechanisms and systems for budget resource allocation, and collaboratively advance reforms in administrative systems, government responsibilities, organizational structures, and mechanisms that empower both central and local government initiatives.

To bolster national governance, it is crucial to fully enforce the Budget Law, emphasizing the development of a comprehensive, uniform, and transparent budget system. This includes refining budget creation and instituting strong decision-making protocols.

Furthermore, it is essential to regulate budget execution, enhance audits and evaluations, foster transparency and public involvement, and reinforce the rational and legal underpinnings of budget management.

Bibliography

Zhu Xi 朱熹. 2016. *Sishu Zhangju Jizhu* 四书章句集注 (Collected Commentaries on the Four Books), specifically *Zhongyong Zhangju* (Commentaries on the Zhongyong), pages 14–41. Beijing: Zhonghua Shuju 中华书局 (Zhonghua Book Company).

Y. Gou, *The Mean in Budgeting*, https://doi.org/10.1007/978-981-96-9592-8

MIX
Papier aus verantwortungsvollen Quellen
Paper from responsible sources
FSC® C105338

If you have any concerns about our products,
you can contact us on
ProductSafety@springernature.com

In case Publisher is established outside the EU,
the EU authorized representative is:
Springer Nature Customer Service Center GmbH
Europaplatz 3, 69115 Heidelberg, Germany

Printed by Libri Plureos GmbH
in Hamburg, Germany